T0279956

A BRIEF LIFE OF
THOMAS AQUINAS

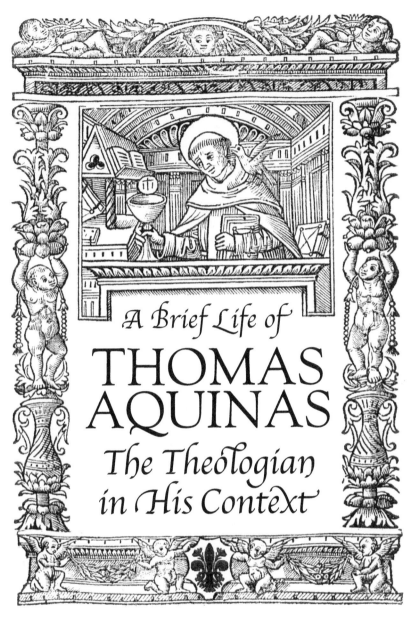

A Brief Life of
THOMAS AQUINAS
The Theologian
in His Context

JEAN-PIERRE TORRELL, OP

Translated by Benedict M. Guevin, OSB

THE CATHOLIC UNIVERSITY OF AMERICA PRESS
WASHINGTON, D.C.

Translation Copyright © 2024
The Catholic University of America Press
All rights reserved

Originally Published as *St. Thomas en plus simple*, © Les Éditions du Cerf, 2019.

The paper used in this publication meets the minimum requirements of
American National Standards for Information Science—
Permanence of Paper for Printed Library Materials, ANSI Z39.48-1992.

Cataloging-in-Publication Data is available from the Library of Congress

ISBN: 978-0-8132-3796-1 | eISBN: 978-0-8132-3797-8

Book design by Burt&Burt
Interior typeset in LTC Goudy, Minion Pro, and Trajan Sans Pro

On the cover and title page: Detail from the "frontespizio" (frontispiece)
of an edition of Thomas Aquinas's *Super libros De Generatione et
Corruptione Aristotelis*, ca. 1520, Lyon, France.
Available through Wikimedia Commons.

CONTENTS

FOREWORD

I f you purchased this book because of its title, this no doubt means that you have already tried to read something by St. Thomas or about him and have decided to stop because of some unforeseen obstacle, like the language was too difficult or you were unaccustomed to it. This first hurdle is not impossible. At the very least you know who St. Thomas is; you have heard others speak of him and desire to know him better. It is enough to maintain this first attitude—what philosophers readily describe as that which is proper to human beings: the desire to know. Without this desire, this little book will be of no use to you. If, however, this desire remains, so too does hope. A little effort is sometimes needed, and so I hope that you will not be disappointed.

Without sacrificing anything of its richness, it is possible to present Thomas's thought in a way accessible to everyone by tracing his life's story. We discover the person behind the writer. He lived a busier life than we could have imagined. Far from being shut up among his books, he travelled the roads of Europe out of holy obedience. He faced a number of important conflicts of ideas as well as situations that he had not chosen, and these clashes gave birth to some of his best-known works. On several occasions, he found himself at the forefront of debates that defined his existence. While he wrote his most famous books against the backdrop of silence, or for years through winds and tides, many of his contemporaries frequently asked for his advice on an incredible variety of subjects. As for the supposed difficulty of reading his texts, allow me to offer something to guide you; then you will see that at least some of those texts are much easier to understand than you might have imagined.

BENE SCRIPSISTI THOMA

EARLY YEARS

L ike many famous authors, Thomas Aquinas is sometimes hidden behind his books. This is unfortunate,
since it is quite possible, and even necessary, to "read"
his life at the same time as his writings, for his life can
shed light on his works with respect to not only their number
or the topics he writes about, but their content as well. Without
making Thomas into a cradle saint, we can learn a lot even from
his early years about his personality and his thought.

Roccasecca, Monte Cassino, Naples
(ca. 1226–1245)

Let us take an example from the family to which Thomas
belonged. What with others might be nothing but anecdotal
bears, in Thomas's case, unexpected interest. We know for a fact

that Aquinas was Italian and that he was born at Roccasecca—in the region near Monte Cassino, just north of Naples and inland--of a noble family. This geographical location ceases to be banal if we are aware that the lands of the family chateau were on both sides of the border that separated the Papal States to the north from the property of the emperor to the south. For better or for worse, the interests and attachments, therefore, were shared and, at times, at odds. The most tragic example is that of Renaud, the second of the family's sons, who placed himself under obedience to Pope Innocent IV. The pope had deposed Emperor Frederick II in 1245; however, when the emperor gained the upper hand, he had Renaud put to death for conspiring against him. Renaud was considered to be a martyr by some of his family, whereas for Frederick and his allies, he was a traitor. It is too soon to draw any conclusions about how Thomas, twenty years old at the time, reacted to this episode. But there is little doubt that his vision of the relations between the temporal and the spiritual, a vision that distinguished him from his contemporaries, had its roots in this drama.

His father, Landolf, and his mother, Theodora, had nine children: five girls, of whom one died young, and four boys. According to the customs of the time, Thomas, being the youngest, was destined for a life in the Church. The proximity of the Abbey of Monte Cassino led to the boy Thomas's being given to the monastery as an oblate, with the ulterior motive that he should one day be made abbot. According to the documents at our disposal, this occurred between July 1230 and May 1231, when Thomas was five or six years old, and, like Saint Benedict, he was accompanied to the monastery by his nurse. There he was initiated into the Benedictine life, traces of which we find in his writings. Without having been, properly speaking, a monk (he was merely an oblate, a simple Christian seeking to live according to the Rule of Saint Benedict), he seems to have had a particular affection for the monastery of his childhood. In fact, near the end of his life, when he was asked to respond to questions from the abbot, he did not hesitate to send his letter with the prompt obedience of a respectful son to his dear father. In fact, Monte Cassino's necrology lists him as a monk of the abbey.

Thomas left the abbey in the spring of 1239 at the age of 13 or 14. Besides his initiation to Benedictine life, he also had a basic solid education. We neither have nor need precise information to be certain of that. His adolescent years simply prove his knowledge not only of letters in the narrow sense of the word (including Latin), but also the quality of what he had learned. His knowledge of Gregory the Great and Cassian, for example, was quite out of the ordinary. Thus, he was able from the outset to enter the university at Naples, which had been founded fifteen years earlier by Frederick II, who needed leaders for his empire. Sicily and southern Italy were then exceptionally supportive of the intellectual life. Already, and for quite some time, Michel Scotus and his team of translators had been working to introduce the Latin world to Greek and Arab knowledge. Philosophy and knowledge of Aristotle, as well as Arab astronomy and Greek medicine, flourished in Palermo, Salerno, and Naples.

Researchers have long searched for the identities of the professors with whom Thomas might have studied; we now realize that we can know nothing with certainty. What is certain, as subsequent events will testify, is that he put to good use what he had learned during these early years. For him, the event that clearly made the most impression on him was the discovery of the Order of Preachers. There was, in fact, a Dominican convent in Naples founded in 1231. Frederick II could barely tolerate these mendicants, whose allegiance to the pope was too close, even if the convent had only two friars. But Thomas discovered in them the ideal of Saint Dominic and decided to join them several years later, receiving the habit in 1244. Thus began the most famous episode in the life of the young Thomas.

His parents no doubt had not abandoned their ambitions that Thomas would one day be the abbot of Monte Cassino. His mother thus decided to get him to change his mind about joining the Order of Preachers. Thomas had already left Naples. The Dominicans of Naples, who had witnessed the pillaging of their convent several years earlier during the clothing of a young noble whose family sought to force him out of the convent, had learned from the experience and sent Thomas to Rome. His mother pursued him there but arrived too late. Thomas had already left for Bologna with other Dominicans accompanying the master of the Order who, himself, was travelling there. Far from being outdone, Lady Theodora quickly sent a letter to her sons who were fighting alongside of Frederick II and charged them with the task of intercepting their brother and returning him to the family home. Their mission was accomplished near Orvieto during the first two weeks of May. We can skip over the details of this chase, which biographers have embellished though the bare facts are already incredible enough. It was easy to capture the young brother, to put him on a horse, and to bring him back to Roccasecca.

This well-known story not only reminds us of the customs of the time, it also has the advantage of illustrating our point and unexpectedly sheds light on the future doctrine of our author. Many years later, when he was speaking about the various obstacles encountered by young people wishing to enter religious life, Thomas appropriately quotes a passage from Saint Jerome, who talks about family, the affection of those close to us, with father and mother in first place. The greatest enemies of the young convert are also the closest. Jerome emphasizes the tears and entreaties of parents, going so far as to insist that if your father is lying down on the road so that you might not pass, you should not hesitate to trample him underfoot. Thomas, who has no fear of using this shocking advice, adds his own words: *as well as your own mother*. After what we have just read, it is difficult not to see in Thomas's words an involuntary personal confidence.

We would be mistaken, however, to imagine that Thomas was badly treated at Roccasecca. He was not in any way relegated to a cell. According to our own categories, he was confined to the house. And if the entire family tried in vain to change his mind, he could come and go within the limits of the property, and he could receive visitors, including repeat visits from his sisters, and from—more astonishing when we think of what had just happened—the Dominicans of Naples, who brought him a new habit to replace the one that had been ripped during his kidnapping. He could pass the time as he wished and, according to his first biographer, who was told this by the family, he used his time to pray, read (or, better, reread) the whole Bible as well as Peter Lombard's *Sentences*, of which he became a preeminent commentator.

This state of affairs lasted a little more than a year. Seeing that nothing would change Thomas's resolve, the family sent him to the Dominican convent in Naples. Among the reasons that may have led to this change of mind, a change in the political situation seems to have played a decisive role. On July 17, 1245, Pope Innocent IV deposed Frederick II; it seems likely that with the change of power the family judged that it would be useful to return to the good graces of the pope, and Thomas was its first beneficiary. It was for this reason that in the autumn of 1245, Thomas returned to Naples. He did not remain there, though, but quickly left for Rome, from which he left not long after to go to Paris in the company of the master of the Order, John the Teuton, who was going there to preside at the General Chapter that was to take place at Pentecost in 1246; and Paris was where Thomas could complete his studies.

This first part of Thomas's life calls for a few remarks. We have to underscore that Thomas did not hold a grudge against his family for having delayed the fulfillment of his desire. That may seem paradoxical, but living in a feudal world as he did (many details show this), he remained very close to his family milieu and his clan. Many witnesses assure us that he had excellent relations with his family members until the end of his life. However, it is more important to return to two points that stand out during this period.

Having seen the overlapping of religion and politics in his family and the reversals of alliances that it had witnessed, we have every reason to believe that Thomas took the duration of his house arrest to meditate on this experience and that he learned from it. In a famous text, written ten years later, in which he speaks of the relationship between ecclesiastical and secular powers, he makes a clear distinction between the domain of temporal power and that of spiritual power:

> Both spiritual power and secular power come from the divine power; this is why secular power is subordinate to spiritual power only to the extent that this submission was God's doing, and that which has to do with the salvation of souls; in this domain, it is better to obey spiritual power rather than secular power. However, when it comes to politics, it is better to obey secular power over spiritual power, according to what we read in Matthew 21:2: "Render to Caesar what is Caesar's."[1]

---

1 All of these anonymous texts are from Thomas himself.

The text does not stop there, nor does Thomas's thought on this subject. What is noteworthy about this passage is that Thomas was the only one at his time to speak like this. Contrary to his contemporaries, Saint Bonaventure or even Saint Albert, still wed to the formula *ecclesia* = *christianitas* (Church and Christianity are the same thing) inherited from the High Middle Ages, with its permanent tension between hierocratism (the superiority of the religious) and caesaropapism (the hegemony of secular power) that ensued, Thomas clearly has a dualistic vision of the relationship between the Church and civil society. On this point, Thomas will never change. If this teaching had been received at that time, this would have spared his family not a few disappointments.

The second point worth noting comes from the stubbornness with which the young Thomas persevered in his choice to become a Dominican. Benedictine life, in which he spent the first years of his life and which left a lasting impact on him, was by no means unworthy of him. Why did he decide on joining a newly-founded religious order (1221) that was little known, poor, and despised by powerful religious organizations that had reigned without challenge for many years, an order that, moreover, could bring no glory to his family? Here we can only speculate, but some conclusions seem obvious. Thomas must have quickly discovered that his penchant for studying and his role in preaching the Gospel would be better satisfied with the Dominicans than with the Benedictines. There were certainly learned men in the Order of Saint Benedict, and there was a rich library at Monte Cassino—one that Thomas would continue to make use of in the years to follow; however, according to the theory that he developed in his more mature years, Thomas had, perhaps, thought that while it is good to contemplate the divine realities, it is better to contemplate them and transmit them in words. There is, nonetheless, another factor at play in Thomas's choice and in his desire to live a life of poverty. As Marie-Dominique Chenu excellently stated, "the refusal of Monte Cassino is, for Thomas, the exact replica of Saint Francis," stripping himself of his rich clothing in the public square of Assisi. The teaching that Thomas would later develop leaves no doubt about what he was thinking. In the dispute that pitted the mendicant friars against the richly endowed secular masters at the University of Paris, Thomas reveals a genuine mysticism concerning poverty:

> Of all things that Christ accomplished or suffered during his earthly life, it is especially the venerable cross that Christians are called to imitate.... Now among the distinctive marks of the cross is absolute poverty: we can see it in exterior things by the fact that he was reduced to complete nakedness.... It is this nakedness of the cross that those who are voluntarily poor follow.... It is clear then that the enemies of poverty are also enemies of the cross (Philippians 3:18).

We are accustomed to praise Thomas Aquinas as a philosopher of great caliber and a theologian without equal. He is, indeed, these things, as we will discover soon enough. But, at the beginning, he wanted nothing more than to be a true religious, desirous of living according to the ideal of poverty of the Friars Preachers. Clearly, his disciples did not always follow in his footsteps, but he remained faithful to his original vocation. It was only thus that he became "Saint" Thomas.

In Paris (1245/46–1248) and Cologne (1248–1251/52)

According to William of Tocco, Thomas's first biographer, the master of the Order "received Thomas at Rome as a dear son in Christ, sending him first to Paris, then to Cologne," to study under Albert the Great. This immediately raises the question: why was Thomas sent to Paris and not to some other city? If it were only a question of distancing him from Naples, this could have been achieved with less expense. What is more, the selection process of brothers judged worthy to study in Paris was very rigorous. There is only one plausible answer. It has to be acknowledged that his intellectual gifts had been noticed very early on, and it was thus that this young brother from a far-off province was sent straightaway to the theological capital of Christendom. It is important to stress this. While in Bologna, the study of law reigned supreme, theology was the queen in Paris, and the Dominicans played a key role. Founded in 1217 as a house of studies for the brothers of the Order of Preachers coming to Paris to study, the first Dominican convent was established in the rue Saint-Jacques in 1218 and quickly became the privileged place for admission to the University. In 1229, Brother Roland of Cremona began teaching as a sitting professor. He was quickly followed by Jean de Saint-Gilles, an English secular professor, who received the Dominican habit in September 1230. As he was already a sitting professor, he kept his chair and continued teaching. Shortly after, he was replaced by Hugh of Saint-Cher and Guerric de Saint-Quentin. Hugh quickly became famous for his biblical work as the head of a team of brothers (a revision of the Bible and concordances, which gathered together references to similar passages) before being named a cardinal. Guerric took over the role of chair in 1233 until his death 1242. A contemporary of the Franciscan master Alexander of Hales, Guerric was the "co-inventor" of the literary genre known as *quodlibets* (a special university exercise that we will see in more detail later). Albert the Great would succeed Guerric and would also become Thomas's master. Thus, Aquinas found himself in a long-established, rich intellectual milieu, with a well-stocked library at his disposal, surrounded by carefully selected students, and under the direction of a well-respected master.

According to the sources available to us, we can date Thomas's arrival in Paris to the end of 1245 or, at the latest, before Pentecost of 1246. He will stay there until 1246 or 1247, and return for the early part of 1248, for a total of three academic years. We cannot exclude the possibility that the first year was spent in the novitiate, which Thomas had not yet done since receiving the habit in April of 1244. But this is not entirely certain. At this time, the period of the novitiate had not yet been fixed; it could be reduced to six months and even ignored altogether, since the brothers could profess vows as soon as they had received the habit.

As for the two subsequent years, we know nothing for certain either. Thomas could have studied philosophy (at what was called the Faculty of Arts at the time), in order to complete the formation that he had begun in Naples between the ages of 14 and 18. A number of indications in his later work witness to his having a good knowledge of the state of philosophy taught at Paris at that time. However, we are more or less certain that he studied philosophy and theology at the same time, the latter under the direction of Albert the Great, for whom he acted as an assistant. Besides, it was with Albert that Thomas left for Cologne in 1248.

The choice to send Thomas to Cologne was in keeping with the earlier choice to send him to Paris. Albert had been sent to Cologne as a result of a decision of the General Chapter that took place at Pentecost that same year. Like Paris, Cologne had had a Dominican convent since 1221 or 1222, and the Chapter charged Albert with the task of establishing a new *studium generale*, a house of studies for graduate-level students that received not only Dominicans but others as well. Thomas was to assist Albert in this task. They both left as soon as classes had ended in Paris, just after June 29. They had already arrived in Cologne for the Feast of the Assumption, and it was entirely possible that Thomas assisted at the laying of the first stone of the cathedral, which took place the same day. In one of his books, Albert speaks of the landscaping undertaken on that occasion as well as the updating of the superb ancient mosaics.

If we exclude various fanciful anecdotes, we know very little of Thomas's schedule during his sojourn in Cologne. In all probability, Thomas was ordained to the priesthood at around this time. His role as Master Albert's assistant and his multiple tasks in assisting other students as part of his position have left very few hints. On the other hand, we can glean from his later works clear traces of the great influence that Albert had on him. During these four years, from the ages of 23 to 27, Thomas became deeply imbued with Albert's thought, for he spent a considerable amount of time preparing Albert's course notes for publication. These notes include *The Celestial Hierarchy* and *The Divine Names*—a Christian adaptation of the teachings of the Neoplatonist Proclus (412–485), of that of Denys (who was confused with Denys the Areopagite, who was converted by Paul in Athens), as well as of Aristotle's *Nicomachean Ethics*. Albert was a zealous worker. He went so far has to write his *Commentary on Ethics* on scraps of paper. It was this work that gave birth to the *Tabula libri Ethicorum*. This little-known work is in the form of a lexicon, the definitions of which, for the most part, are almost verbatim quotations of Albert. René-Antoine Gauthier suggests that Thomas could have undertaken its writing at the same time as he was working on the Second Part of the *Summa* (in 1271). If he left this work (the *Tabula libri Ethicorum*) unfinished, this could be due to the fact that his level of maturity (he would not wait long before undertaking his own *Commentary on Ethics*) would have allowed him to notice the imperfections in the work of his former master.

This stay in Cologne marks the end of the period of Thomas's formation. Following a formula that would become dear to him, it was now his turn to give to others what he himself had received. For this, he had to return to Paris.

BENESCRIPSISTI THOMA·

COMMENTARIES ON ISAIAH AND SENTENCES

Consulted by the master of the order regarding a new professor whom he could send to Paris, Master Albert suggested Thomas. John of Falkenberg seems to have hesitated, but the intervention of Cardinal Hugh of Saint-Cher, a former professor at Paris, supported Albert's choice. Thus Thomas left for Paris in 1252 or 1253 to prepare himself to "read"—we would say to "teach"—or, more exactly, to comment on Lombard's *Sentences*. This preparation involved a prior step: before becoming a "bachelor of the *Sentences*" (we will explain what this title means shortly), the future candidate for the master's had to read the Bible cursively for a year (the task of the "biblical bachelor"). This method consisted of going through a book of the Bible and giving a summary of it to one's beginning students without spending time on a detailed commentary. This would come later, once one had become a master of theology.

THE COMMENTARY ON ISAIAH

At the start of his teaching career, Thomas chose to write on the prophets Isaiah and Jeremiah. Regarding Isaiah, this work published after his death has considerable interest from several points of view. To begin with, it is the first book of our author and at the same time one of the first examples of this type of cursive teaching by a religious. Then, Thomas's choice for the literal meaning of the Bible in preference to its allegorical sense is already asserted here, even if this means upsetting certain traditional interpretations—to the extent that some people have even gone so far as to suspect its authenticity. But as it happens, there is no doubt about Thomas's authorship, since a good part of his manuscript has come down to us in the form of an autograph, written in his well-known "unreadable" hand (for a long time, some had called it "unintelligible," but this was due to a misreading of the text). We cannot help but rejoice at this characteristic of Thomas's writing style, since the study of this autograph allows us to read Thomas as he is preparing his text, in the process of preparing for his course, with its hesitations, its corrections, its repetitions, and, finally, the final state of his thoughts. A close study of this autograph also reveals the character of our author. We will come back to this later.

In addition to the commentary on Isaiah itself, the most characteristic feature of this work is found in the marginal annotations that accompany the text. It is as if Thomas had jotted them down for himself alone so as not to forget them, incidental ideas that came into his head. Without referring directly to the literal teaching properly understood, these marginalia are still a part of the commentary, since they reveal the spiritual or mystical sense of the text. These "collations," as we call them, are short collections of brief biblical citations used with respect to a word found in the biblical text. To get a better idea of what this looks like, it will be helpful to show the reader one of these collations. This will allow us to understand not only how Thomas worked, but also the richness of these numerous overlooked short texts. These texts are of particular interest in highlighting Thomas's spirituality.

Concerning Isaiah 49:17: "I teach you useful things," Thomas writes:

The Word of God is useful for:

Enlightening the mind (Proverbs 6:23): "Teaching is a light";

Rejoices the senses (Psalm 119:103): "His promise is sweet to my taste";

enflaming the heart (Jeremiah 20:9): "It was in my heart as a devouring fire": (Psalm 105:19): "The Word of the Lord enflames";

make straight one's path, Psalm 25:4: "Guide me in your truth and teach me";

obtaining glory, Proverbs 3:21: "Preserve sound judgment and discretion";

teaching others, 2 Timothy 3:16: "All scripture is inspired and is useful for teaching, refuting…

This collation is a well-structured meditation on the place of God's Word in theology and preaching. Since we lack the space to allow us to develop this exceptionally rich theme, we should at least recognize that these annotations, these spiritual extensions full of the experience of the prophets and the wise, the apostles and evangelists, show us the biblical timbre of Thomas's spirituality. When reading them, we are also struck by what captivated Thomas in these texts and therefore his attitude before God and the Word. For example, in the passage cited above, we can glimpse in particular the sensitivity of this friar preacher or, in other words, his soul of an apostle and a saint. This information is priceless in light of Thomas's known natural reserve, a reserve that seldom allows us to discover the man hidden behind the words of the text. Hyacinthe-François Dondaine expressed this well when he wrote, "it is only by means of the manuscript of the *Super Isaiam* that one can participate—in the margins of the literal commentary—in this outpouring of the *collationes*, with their interplay of sacred texts exposing the univocity of the *historia*." We will come back to this when we speak about the four senses of Scripture.

Bachelor of the *Sentences*

Thomas began his teaching of the *Sentences* in September of the academic year 1251–1252 or 1252–1253. This was the second step in his preparation for the master's degree of theology. According to an often-used comparison, a bachelor's commentary on the *Sentences* is like a masterpiece that the apprentice had to present in order to become a master. Between teaching strictly speaking and the definitive redaction, the completion of his commentary on Peter Lombard's *Sentences* will take Thomas approximately four years. Actually, Thomas will teach and write at the same time, with the result that his commentary on Book I had already been published even before he had finished teaching Book III, and Thomas will not complete Book IV until he had already received the master's degree.

The *Book of Sentences*, written by Peter Lombard, who had taught at Paris a century earlier (1155–1158), had been introduced into the university's curriculum by Alexander of Hales, who was the first to use this book as the basis for his teaching (1223–1227). Lombard's book would remain an obligatory part of the theology curriculum for three centuries. For better or for worse, all of the Scholastics had to be formed in this mold. In Thomas's time, the *Sentences* was part of the three foundational books that the superiors had to provide for the brothers destined for further studies. The other two were the Bible and the Peter Comestor's *Historia scholastica* (1179).

The title, *Book of Sentences*, comes from its content. Peter Lombard had wanted to gather together in one work the different opinions (*sententiae*) of the Fathers of the Church on diverse theological topics, and he quoted mostly from the texts themselves for the convenience of both the masters and the students. Usually limited to commentaries, theologians did not believe that they were obligated to follow this strict format. Thomas was neither the first nor the only one to go beyond Peter Lombard's work, and he often presented his own commentary on the text in a breadth unknown to its first author, who, nonetheless, was always referred to as "the Master" (*magister*). Thus, we can consider Thomas's commentary, as well as those of all of the other commentators, as fully theological works. Thus, the characteristics of Thomas's commentary reveal the direction of the young professor. As a result, we can consider as significant the 2,034 citations from Aristotle in Thomas's commentary—the most quoted of all of the pagan writers—or the 1,095 citations from Augustine—way ahead of all of the other Christian writers he cites, who are already highly represented (with 3,000 Christian citations in total).

Still, more than this quantitative data, the difference between Thomas and Lombard is the way in which Thomas, from the very first pages of his commentary, expresses his understanding of theology. It is clear from the way each expresses himself that, on the one hand, the four books of Lombard are above all a collection of citations tied together loosely around the general theme of each book: (1) God, (2) God as Creator, (3) The incarnation of the Word, (4) the sacraments. Thomas, on the other hand, is not content with simply listing citations; rather, he seeks to uncover what he calls the *intentio* of the Master and sets out to organize the whole of theology, with God as its center and everything else surrounding God, according to the relationship that they have with Him: either as the first source of their origin, or as their final end.

Even though this schema is simple in appearance, it takes on new meaning if we recall the biblical affirmation of God as the Alpha and the Omega of all things visible and invisible, and if, moreover, one follows Thomas, who joins together this circular movement with the intimate relationships that the three Persons of the Trinity have from all eternity as the fundamental reason for this movement. In fact, the "exit" of creatures from God as the first source finds its meaning in the truth that, even in God, there is an exit from the Father that we call the "generation" or emanation of the Word, the second Person of the Trinity. The divine efficiency exercised in the creation is thus related to the generation of the Word. In the same way, the causality of grace, which makes possible the successful return of creatures to God by means of the movement of the Holy Spirit, is connected to the return of the Word to the Father. In the language that we find, God's action in our world is exterior to God, so to speak, and cannot be understood except in the light of the intra-divine fecundity. Everything comes from God and returns to God in a way that is incomprehensible to us.

There are many other things we could retain from this commentary on the *Sentences* but, for the moment, we can note the first thing. Without saying everything, Thomas's commentary contains a profound spiritual intuition for whoever wishes to penetrate his thought. It would be simple to show that he arranges things such that his own commentary replicates this vision of things. But Thomas's commentary is more than a simple pedagogical option; it is a rich theological intuition that already anticipates the outline of the *Summa theologiae*. This has two major implications. First, attentive to the meaning of the word *theo*-logy, Thomas sees in God himself the first "subject" of his work. If Thomas deals with the Word Incarnate only after this—for which others will reproach him—it is because he gives first place to the Trinity: no more than the creation, the Incarnation cannot be explained by itself; one has to go back to love as its source, the Father of light from whom come all perfect gifts. Next, we have to underscore that, according to this view, the entire universe of creatures, spiritual and material, are animated with a basic power that, when the time comes, will allow for the effortless integration of historical development within theological reflection.

BENESCRIPSISTI THOMA·

MASTER OF
SACRED SCRIPTURE

B y definition, the role of bachelor was transitional.
From February 1256, Aymeric de Veyre, the chancellor
of the university, granted Thomas the permission to
teach (*licentia docendi*) and ordered him to prepare
the inaugural lecture. Thomas presented this lecture sometime
between March 3 and 17 of 1256. The different phases of the
investiture ceremony were held over two days and were hardly a
formality. Given the public and adversarial nature of the debates
that were a part of this ceremony, the position of the newcomer
was "uncomfortable" to the very end. We have preserved copies
of two of Thomas's main interventions for this occasion, and
they deserve to be known better. Nevertheless, it would be more
profitable for us to follow Thomas's thinking under three aspects

of his new functions. These had been laid out by Peter Cantor at the beginning of the century: *legere* (read), *disputare* (discuss), *praedicare* (preach).

"Read": Commenting on the Bible

For those who consider Thomas to be only a philosopher, or who have not consulted the *Summa theologiae*, it may come as a surprise that the first task of a master of theology, which is what Thomas was then, was to comment on the Bible. Unlike the more cursive reading, the only kind that a bachelor was allowed to do (for example, Thomas's comments on the *Book of Isaiah*), the kind of teaching reserved to the master allowed him to do a more in depth commentary, as Thomas will do on the Book of Job and the Gospel according to John. Because Thomas is better known as the author of the *Commentary on the Sentences* and the *Summa theologiae*, it is not well-known that his commentaries on the Bible were his daily task as a professor. If, therefore, we want to have a less one-sided understanding of the complete theologian that Thomas was, we must keep in mind his biblical teaching. All the rest of his works, in spite of their ampler size, were written in addition to his ordinary work as a professor. Thus, after having commented on *Isaiah* and *Jeremiah* while he was a bachelor, Thomas, as a master, commented on the *Book of Job* and the first fifty-three psalms, the Gospels according to Matthew and John, and on all of the letters of St. Paul. This prodigious work, with its astonishing wealth of content, has now been almost entirely translated and has been the object of a great deal of scholarship. We highly recommend reading them (at least occasionally). In addition, we are surprised to find, in reading these texts, that they undergird Thomas's public discourse as well as his preaching.

For his first teaching, Thomas chose to comment on the *Gospel according to Matthew*. We cannot go into detail about this commentary, but from the outset we are struck by its more spontaneous charm, in comparison with his more formal written works. Thus, we find allusions to the place where he is living, in France, in Paris, or to current events in theology. This is not by accident. This commentary, which has come to us in the form of hasty course notes, has kept something of the oral style of the master who did not have the time to revisit his course to make it more polished. We can also see that Thomas's choice for the literal meaning of the commentary on *Isaiah* is, in fact, affirmed in his other scriptural works. This means not only that the literal meaning is the only one adaptable to the necessities of theological argumentation, but also that all spiritual interpretation must be based on the literal meaning in order to avoid the risk of error. The literal meaning of scripture is not only not an occasionally necessary hindrance to a spiritual interpretation, since, for Thomas, the spiritual interpretation is already found in the letter of scripture. This also leads Thomas to the awareness of the limits of allegorical exegesis, which, until then, had been widely practiced.

To arrive at a more precise idea of how Thomas understands this, we will cite a single and exceptionally rich passage from his exegesis on Matthew: an explanation of the temptations of Jesus in the desert. Thomas discusses the meaning of temptation in general and that of each of the temptations in particular. He explores their interior reality in order to determine how they can be applied to Christ, and the role that the temptations play in the whole of the Gospel, on their importance for the mission of Jesus and for us, and so forth. Here, he is at the midpoint between theology and spirituality (if it were possible to distinguish the two!). He is also interested in what we would call the exegesis of Satan, that is, the way in which Satan twists the meaning of the verses of scripture in order to apply them falsely to Christ. In doing this, Thomas is, at the same time, giving us a lesson in exegesis.

> Note that one can improperly interpret a verse of scripture in three ways. First, when it is a question of one thing being applied to another, e.g., when one speaks about a just person and uses it to talk about Christ, e.g., "He could have sinned but he did not" (Sirach 31:10), or again, "the Father is greater than me" (John 14:28); this is said of Christ as a man, but if one applies this to Christ in his quality of Son of God, one has improperly interpreted the verse. Here, what the devil says of angels: "They will bear you in their hands lest you strike your foot against a stone," is applied to a just man, a member of Christ, who, in fact, has need of the angels so that he does not sin; this cannot be applied to Christ, who is sinless.
>
> A second way to interpret scripture falsely is to use a verse and apply it to someone to whom it is not directed. Thus Proverbs 25:21 and Romans 12:20: "If an enemy is hungry, then feed him, and you will heap burning coals on his head." If someone does this in view of seeing God punish him, this is against the meaning of the verse. The devil does likewise: when scripture assures that the just will be guarded by angels in such a way that he will not be endangered . . . , the devil is suggesting that man should expose himself to danger, which is tempting God.
>
> The third way consists in retaining from a verse that which goes our way and rejecting that which does not. This is what the heretics do. This is what the devil is doing here since he omits the end of the citation, which is contrary to what he is asserting: "On the venomous snake and the viper you will walk, and trample the lion and the dragon." This is why the devil has become the prototype of those who misinterpret scripture.

"Disputation":
Disputed Questions on the Truth

The second function of a master of theology was what we call *disputatio*. Disputation is still teaching but with a different form: it is an active teaching method that proceeds by way of objections and answers on a specific theme. For example, a commentary on scripture sometimes raised questions to which the master did not always have the time to respond. So the master would customarily treat these questions separately and would submit them for further discussion in circumstances where the participants—more often than not the students—would raise arguments for and against in order to appreciate better the interest and importance of the question raised. After the discussion, the master would synthesize the exchange and provide his own answer. If the question was important enough to call for a more prolonged treatment, the master could split it up into smaller pieces, called "articles," that one could deal with in a single class period. Very quickly this form of teaching was no longer left to random simple questions raised during class time. Rather, it was the master himself who, at the beginning of the academic year, proposed subjects to be treated in addition to his regular teaching.

The disputation was made up of two essential forms. The first, private (*disputatio privata*), took place within the school with only the master's students and his bachelor. The second, which was public (*disputatio publica* or *ordinaria*), the masters had to hold on a regular basis. Often many professors would not participate because of the perilous nature of such public disputations. The public disputations, in contrast to the private, could be attended by students and sometimes masters of other schools could participate. Once in a while, these masters could not hold back and made it a point to embarrass the master who was conducting the disputation. In one of its forms, the second type of disputed questions could even be a solemn event (the famous *Quodlibets* about which we will speak later) that was held twice a year, once during Advent and once during Lent, and which would interrupt the regular classes at the University.

To have some idea of what the private disputes between Thomas and his students could be like, we can lay out the teaching schedule at Saint-Jacques in the following way: at the first hour of the day, very early, Thomas would teach; after he finished, the bachelor would take over; in the afternoon, both Aquinas and his bachelor would gather with their students to "dispute" a chosen theme. The three hours given over to this active pedagogy would not always be sufficient time to exhaust the subject, since the process required going through it article by article. Eventually, certain very short articles could be dealt with together in one meeting while, by contrast, a longer or more delicate subject could be broken up over several meetings. The result (objections, responses, and authoritative determinations) were then assembled into a final version of the question and prepared for publication. This was how, for example, the refinement of the questions *On Truth* (*De veritate*) was spread out over the first three academic years (1256–1259) at the rate of eighty articles per year. This corresponds closely to the number of teaching days per year.

If this framework corresponds to reality, we should nevertheless add two indispensable complements. First, it is likely that the final result that has come down to us is far from the actual unfolding of these disputes between the master and his students. It is sufficient to read the text of the questions *On Truth* to understand that the tenor of these texts is way above what an average student could contribute to a discussion. The students at Paris, who were better formed than those of Rome later on, could undoubtedly follow more difficult lectures. Nevertheless, even their discussions could not have taken on the exact form of these long, complex, and deeply researched subjects. By necessity, they were shorter and simpler. We have to admit that what has come down to us gives witness to a considerable redactional work on the part of the master. Next, one has to know that in Thomas's day, the *Disputed Questions* had for a long time become a literary genre. Formed in the dialectic of *pro* and *contra*, the minds of this era readily expressed themselves using this form; the best example of this is the *Summa theologiae*, which is composed using this method throughout. And we could multiply the examples.

If we now come to the content, *On Truth* is an imposing work that contains 253 articles grouped into 29 questions that can be further divided into two large subsets: (1) truth and knowledge (qq. 1–20); and (2) the good and the desire for the good (qq. 21–29). Listing all of the topics treated would hardly get us anywhere, but we can pause for a moment on the first question and on the two interesting considerations that they awaken, for they shed light on a proper understanding of Thomas's thought. The first is suggested by the title itself, for it reveals Thomas's understanding of the theological project. For it should be stated that several of his works begin with the mention of truth. Truth is literally the first word of the *Summa contra Gentiles*, which we will look at later on: "The truth, this is what my mouth proclaims . . ."—what follows deserves to be known, since the author identifies himself as having come to witness to the truth. For its part, the *Summa theologiae* begins with a similar declaration: "Since the doctor of Catholic truth has as his task. . . ." Given that in Thomas's thought everything is explained from the end that one pursues, it is important to have an idea of that end from the outset. And since the choice of the means depends on the end that one desires to achieve, we can better understand that it is not accidental that three of his major works begin with the word *truth*. It is the truth of the faith that he wants to grasp and understand, expand and defend. It is truth that he wants to spread so that it can be better known and better loved. If one desires to enter into Thomas's thought, this is a path that cannot be neglected.

The second suggestion that we can take from this first article of *On Truth* comes from its content. Not only does Thomas deal with truth, but also with what we call the "transcendentals," those over-arching universally linked qualities of being in general. With the exception of God, who identifies Himself ineffably with Truth, truth is not a reality that exists in itself; rather, it is a property of something that exists (philosophers succinctly and accurately refer to this "something that exists" as "being"). It is the same for similar properties, which, before they come together under various titles to a state in which all beings participate, exist in the being in itself as properties that are inseparably tied to it and are convertible with it and with all of the others. In other words, the first being is not only true, it is before all else something that, depending on how we look at it, presents this or that property. Without looking at all of them, it is easy to understand that, with respect to intelligence, being appears as true and capable of being known, and therefore the truth of our knowledge will be verified in its exactness, in its conformity to reality. Similarly, in its relation to the will—the other important faculty of our soul—being appears as good and, therefore, desirable and worthy of being loved. To the extent that it is in accord with reason and the will, we can say that being appears beautiful. This obtains for all of the other general modes of being considered in themselves or in distinction from other beings. It is always the same being, but we refer to it differently according to the point of view from which we are looking at it. This is why we say that that there is between being and each of its general properties a real identity and a difference that is only "notional", that is, from the point of view from which we are looking at it. This is the reason why we say that between being and its modalities and between modalities themselves, there is a mutual convertibility. To the extent that it is a participant in being, each being is itself something that is one, beautiful, true, and so forth. This is the first intuition to keep in mind: being is, non-being is not, and if being is, each being participates in its overall modes.

There are a lot of other things we could say about the questions *On Truth* and about their importance in Thomas's work, especially with respect to grasping the young Thomas's evolution during these three years. On certain points, he had already changed his position with respect to the *Sentences*, and will do so again in later works. But one must not forget: if Thomas is consistent with himself and his overarching theological enterprise, he is not a rigid systematician but more like a genius in motion, in an act of perpetual discovery. Without going deeper down this path, I would like to share with the reader a particularly telling passage that describes Thomas's state of mind as he works and in which he invites us to share:

> The study (*studium*) of wisdom [one could easy also say: of truth] has the privilege that pursuing its end is sufficient in itself.... As such, the contemplation of wisdom is comparable to a game for two reasons. First, because a game is delightful and that the contemplation of wisdom brings with it supreme delight.... Second, because a game has no other aim than itself and finds in itself its own end; this is what one discovers in the delight of wisdom.... Contrariwise from what happens in our usual pleasures regarding what

we anticipate, where the shortest delay can really spoil our fun . . . , it is in itself that the contemplation of wisdom finds the source of its delight. Consequently, it suffers absolutely no distress when we have to wait for something. . . . This is why divine wisdom compares its own delight to that of a game: "I was filled with delight day after day, rejoicing always in his presence" (Proverbs 8:30).

"Preaching": Theology and Pastoral Ministry

We are so used to seeing Thomas Aquinas as the man of the *Summa theologiae* that many people are astonished to hear about his preaching. And yet, preaching was the third and final task of a master at this time, and Thomas does not fail us. People in the Middle Ages saw no opposition between teaching the science of theology and its extension into the pastoral realm. On the contrary, teaching was seen as the normal preparation for preaching. Peter Cantor was clear about this: "It is after the *lectio* of Scripture and after the examination of unclear points raised in the *disputatio*, and not before, that one should preach."

The masters took care of this aspect of things and strove to make available to pastors not only the "tools of the trade," such as concordances, in order to make the use of the biblical text easier and more reliable, but also their own *lectio* of entire sermons or summaries of sermons in order to aid their hearers to move from *lectio* to *praedicatio*. The masters themselves, of course, knew very well how to use their own tools when it came to preaching. Thus, for the purpose of preaching, Thomas used patristic texts that he had assembled in the *Catena aurea*, about which we will speak later.

This practice shows that the system foreseen by the statutes of the faculty was indeed honored. Even before presenting oneself for the exams for the license, the young theologian had to promise to present personally two *collationes* to the University, or else a *sermo*: both as a homily at Mass and as a *collatio* at Vespers. Once a master, he was still not dispensed from preaching. The statues even provided for the creation of a commission, made up of four masters who were still teaching and heads of schools (master regents, we would say), charged with assigning to others the sermons that they would have to preach during the course of the school year. It was even planned that, if the master could not fulfill his preaching assignment himself, he would have to find another master to replace him. The duty of preaching was not restricted to Sundays alone, but also included feast day preaching to the faculty of theology. In this case, the preaching was done by the mendicants, either the Friars Minor or the Dominicans.

The statutory requirements were increased for Thomas because he was also a Friar Preacher. He must have had to preach at least several times a year in front of the University. These university sermons are less known than his preaching outside of the university context. We have entire series of sermons on the Lord's Prayer, the Ave Maria, the Creed, or the Decalogue, which were highly successful. While each of these four series is attested to by at least eighty manuscript witnesses (or, in the case of the Credo, 150), there are no university sermons that go beyond four manuscript witnesses, and often we have only one manuscript witness.

We have preserved enough of these university sermons (around twenty) that we have a pretty good idea what Thomas's style was and sometimes even the circumstances surrounding some of them. The most picturesque is dated to April 6, 1259.

On that day, Palm Sunday, the beadle of Picardy, named Guillot, took it upon himself to interrupt Thomas while he was in the middle of preaching, in order to make public "before the clergy and the people," the attack of William of Saint-Amour against the mendicants. The incident could have been comical if it had not happened in a stressful situation about which we will speak later. As we can guess from the details, some of these university sermons were a call to arms; however, the tone changed when he was speaking to the simple faithful. So as Thomas was commenting on the Creed and listed the number of reasons why Christ descended into hell, he says:

> The second reason was to come to the aid of his friends in the most perfect way, for he had friends not only in this world but in hell as well. Indeed, we are friends of Christ if we have charity; now there were a lot of people in hell who had died believing in and loving the One who was to come, like Abraham, Isaac, Jacob, Moses, David, and still others who were just and perfect. It was thus that Christ, after having visited his own who were in the world, desired to visit his own who were in hell and come to their aid by going down to them.

To my knowledge, this kind of argument is rarely used; however, it is quite in keeping with an author who will elsewhere draw on his esteem for human friendship in order to speak about our relationship with God. Because this part of Thomas's work is not well known, it is all the more precious in order to understand Thomas better. Unlike a number of his contemporaries, he sets himself apart by his simplicity and sobriety, by the absence of scholastic subtleties and technical words. This attitude of sobriety was not restricted only to fancy words; he also refuses to engage in oratory flourishes. If Thomas knew that the orators needed an art that would stir their listeners, he refused to reduce this art to the wisdom of the world. This is the reason why we do not find in Thomas the funny little stories (*exempla*) so loved by many preachers. He is careful to avoid "frivolities" (*frivolitates*).

For example, in his response to Gerard, the conventional lector at Besançon, who had asked him about the shape of the star that appeared to the wise men (a cross, a man, or a crucifix?), Thomas responds that there is nothing in Scripture or the Tradition that supports this, and he adds, somewhat drily, "It is not fitting for a preacher of truth to lead people astray with unverifiable tales." From the point of view of an intellectual, Thomas's preaching seems astonishingly concrete, based on daily experiences, concerned with social justice and honesty in business. We can certainly glimpse the mentality of Thomas's listeners at this time: superstitious, anti-Semitic, misogynistic, and so forth. Thomas's preaching is rich in citations from the Bible and makes evident a profound love for the word of God (it is in the context of a sermon on respecting Sunday that the Jews are given as an example to Christians, for they spend the Sabbath meditating on Scripture).

As for the content, this preaching takes up many themes from preachers of all times: love of God, devotion to the Virgin Mary, prayer, and humility (Thomas liked the theme of the "little old woman," la *vetula*, who, in her humility, knows more about God than the proud scholar). We also find major themes in his preaching. First, a care for the essential, charity: "The entire law of Christ is found in charity." Then, the imitation of Christ: "All that the Lord did and suffered in his flesh is a healing example and teaching for us." The theme of man as the image of God finds its place in this context, for Christ came to restore this image, which had been disfigured by sin. Here, Thomas insists on freedom as the privileged sign of our divine resemblance.

Finally, he strongly underscores the place of the Holy Spirit as the source of Christian freedom, the bond of ecclesial communion, the source of our prayer, and the guarantor of our requests to the Father.

The abundance of these themes and the way they are treated allows us to see the continuity between teaching properly understood, pastoral theology, and spirituality. There is no break when Thomas moves from the professor's chair to that of the preacher. His spiritual doctrine is a necessary and implicit dimension of his theology. He is not only a thinker and a master of thought, but a master of how to live, as well.

BENESCRIPSISTI THOMA·

THE MAN
OF COMBAT

O ne could conclude that the completion of the redaction of the *Commentary on the Sentences* and the beginning of teaching the questions *De veritate* would have been enough to keep Thomas busy during these years. But such was not the case. To these two major works we should add three other writings that, while shorter, cannot be ignored—*On Being and Essence* (*De ente et essentia*), *The Principles of Nature* (*De principiis naturae*), and *Commentary on the "De Trinitate" of Boethius* (*Super Boetium De Trinitate*)—as well as his defense of *Quodlibets* VIIIX and especially the publication of a not very well known polemical work, *Against the Enemies of the Worship of God and the Religious State* (*Contra Impugnantes Dei cultum et religionem*).

Let us pause for a minute on this last title and recall the context that elicited its writing. It all started in 1230 with the arrival of mendicants, Franciscans and Dominicans, at the University of Paris. Founded at around 1150, the University could count among its most prestigious members Peter Lombard, and, at the time of Thomas, the number of chairs of theology were still limited: twelve in total, of which three were reserved by law to the canons of Notre Dame. When two of these chairs, Roland of Cremona and Jean de Saint-Gilles, joined the Dominicans, followed by a third one, Alexander of Hales, who joined the Franciscans, followed by a fourth, Bonaventure of Bagnoregio, the number and influence of secular chairs diminished, while the competition between masters and paying students increased, often attracted to the novelty of the friars' teaching.

We can skip the nasty squabbles that pepper this story and the difficulties that the newcomers had to endure—who, by the way, gave as good as they got. We can scarcely imagine the violence of this quarrel. During the winter of 1255–56, the friars were assaulted in the streets and their residence Saint Jacques had to be guarded by the king's archers. When Thomas gave his inaugural lecture, it was under their protection, and the rioters prevented those from outside the walls of the university from coming to listen to it. This state of affairs had been going on for more than twenty years when Thomas, who, even though he had been a master since 1256, was not admitted to the faculty until August 15, 1257, and then only through the intervention of the pope. Bonaventure, who was in the same situation, had to wait four years.

Defender of the Religious Life

This struggle entered its doctrinal phase in March–April 1256, with the publication of Guillaume de Saint-Amour's work entitled: *Treatise on the Perils of the End Times*, in which he denounced the new preachers by putting them in the same category as Gerardo de Borgo San Donnino, a Franciscan mystic whose own Order did not hesitate to condemn him. Without hesitation, Thomas got involved in the melée and quickly got to work on refuting Guillaume, and he was able to publish his *Against the Enemies* between May and September of that same year, 1256.

At first glance, this is not one of Thomas's most passionate books; but if we look at it more closely, it is possible to discover things of significant interest. As the title suggests, the book is essentially about defining what a religious order is and establishing the rights of religious to teach and to belong to the professorial class. Thomas also defends their right to preach and to hear confessions even if they are not involved in pastoral ministry and without being hampered by the obligation of manual labor. This is why Thomas reserves for religious the right to the most absolute poverty and especially the possibility to live from almsgiving, so that they would not be mired in the administration of finances or in other matters. Likewise, Thomas tries to demonstrate the iniquity of defamatory accusations leveled at "mendicant religious."

It would be tiresome simply to run through this imposing work, but one can appreciate it from several perspectives. Some are content with praising Thomas's sense of history, in contrast to the static view of Guillaume or the confused messianism of Gerardo. One must especially highlight that we find in the first superb chapter a worthy vision of the religious life. At the root of the religious life, Thomas places the Christian spiritual life in all of its fullness: faith, first of all, which is the first bond that attaches humans to God, as well as hope and charity. Indeed, all of the works of charity become the matter of this "service" rendered to God in the religious life. What unifies all of this is what the New Testament calls a spiritual sacrifice: the offering of oneself, body and soul, as the sweet odor of a victim presented to God (see Romans 12:1), by the vows of chastity and obedience and the renunciation of one's possessions by means of the vow of poverty.

From this, given the expansion of charity to all of the works of the Christian life, it is easy for Thomas to show that there is no work of mercy (in the strong sense that he gives to this word) that cannot be the object of a religious order, *even if it has not been done until now*. The only thing remaining is to assert that preaching and the teaching of theology are works of spiritual mercy ("Teaching is an act of mercy") in order to legitimize at the same time the right of religious to teach as in the case of the Order of Preachers in spite of the novelty of what Thomas says.

After Guillaume's condemnation by the Roman authorities and the retraction of his associates, the debate calmed down for several years, and Thomas could finish his first teaching assignment in a more peaceful atmosphere. This being said, the calm was precarious: without the need to go over this period, let us anticipate a little the rest of the story, for a new wave soon came to assault the religious. Leading the charge was Gerard d'Abbeville. A very active member of the faculty, Gerard was one of the rare masters who, with Thomas, regularly held his two yearly *quodlibet* sessions. Guillaume, richly endowed with benefices, a real "prince of the Church," can be considered to be one of the founders of the Sorbonne library, since he left to the University, founded by his friend Robert de Sorbon, more than three hundred volumes. An adversary of the mendicants until his death, he specified that if he left his books to poor students, it was only on condition that they could not be a religious.

We can skip the details of this new confrontation, but it is possible that the rise in this animosity had been one of the reasons why Thomas returned to Paris in the autumn of 1268, a move that we will speak about shortly. From the spring of 1269, Thomas will once again take up the task of his *Quodlibet* at Easter and, at the same time, write his *Perfection of the Spiritual Life* (*De perfection spiritualis vitae*). Much shorter than his *Against the Enemies*, this work is full of flavor, which makes it easy to read. We can say without hesitation that this is a jewel of spiritual literature. It is also an important step in the development of Thomas's thought regarding the doctrine of the sacrament of orders.

A third work of literary polemic appeared during this period: according to its conclusion, it is directed "against the erroneous and pernicious teaching of those who deter men from entering into religious life," that is, *Against Those Who Lead Astray* (*Contra doctrina retrahentium a religione*, or *Contra Retrehentes*). Essentially, this work forbade the possibility of receiving very young boys and having them take vows. The author returns with insistence to the themes that are dear to him: the primacy of charity and voluntary poverty and a mendicant lifestyle. This was not the heart of the argument, but the one that was the most obvious. Thomas defends one of the newest aspects of his Order and devotes the longest of his chapters to this issue. Still, it is not poverty itself that he deems the most essential:

> If we examine carefully the words of the Lord, it is not even in the giving up of riches that he situates perfection; he only shows it as a path that leads to it; this can be seen even in the way he speaks when he says: "If you wish to be perfect, go, sell

all you have, give it to the poor *and follow me*" (Mt 19:21). Here, he means to say that perfection is found in following Christ and that the renunciation of wealth leads us on this path.

One can guess that it is no longer seculars who are being targeted here, but the Franciscans; what is more, the Franciscans did not misunderstand him, and they violently attacked Thomas's position that poverty was simply a means of arriving at the ideal of the religious life. Thomas thus freed his Order from the endless arguments that continued to disturb the diverse Franciscan currents regarding perfect poverty. We should especially take note in these texts of the place given to "follow Christ." Thomas reveals in these pages a personal mystical connection to the poor Christ, which can be explained in part by the struggles that he had to endure to enter this religious family. In addition to these struggles, his theory of the superiority of the apostolic life over the merely contemplative life is directly based on the example that Christ left to us. Paradoxically, he even maintains that Christ chose this life because of its superiority:

> The contemplative life is better than the active life whose only concerns are bodily necessities, but the active life that consists in bringing to others the preaching and teaching of truths that one has contemplated is more perfect than the contemplative life alone, for it presupposes a fullness of contemplation. And this is why Christ chose this sort of life.

After Christ, the supreme reference is that of the first Church. Thomas, a faithful heir to the successive kinds of religious life which took as their model the early apostolic community (*vita apostolica*), repeats that it is in the primitive Church that one finds the most perfect of religious states. In the face of the arguments of Guillaume de Saint-Amour, who aggressively raised to the level of a juridical law the example of the primitive

Church against the "innovations" of the mendicant orders, he provided the new orders the scriptural basis that assured the legitimacy of their foundation. If this was the kind of life led by the apostles, it is clear that one can follow it in a religious order founded for that purpose.

> All religious orders were founded on the model of the apostolic life, as we read in Acts: "They held everything in common.... The apostolic life was such that having abandoned everything they went out into the world to evangelize and preach, as we see in Mt 10, where this was imposed on them as a rule. One can therefore very well start a religious order with these two tasks.

A Master of Polemics

Let us recall that our purpose is to introduce Thomas Aquinas's thought without forgetting the person. Now these latter books are among those that capture best the passionate side of his temperament. He lacked neither vigor, nor firmness, nor even (as M. Dufeuil has pointed out) at times a "sarcastic irony [that] bursts forth from time to time" in *Against the Enemies*. Thus, when confronted with Guillaume de Saint-Amour, who objected that one could not belong to two schools at the same time (as a master and as a religious), Thomas replies that though Church law does not forbid this, it certainly does forbid belonging simultaneously to two ecclesiastical schools: one cannot be a canon of two different churches. This was precisely the case with Guillaume.

On this point, it is enlightening to reread the conclusion of *The Perfection of the Spiritual Life*, which ends with a blatant challenge:

> If someone wishes to write contrary to this work, this would be most agreeable to me; in fact, truth is never seen better than in resisting those who contradict it and in refuting their error, as it is written in Proverbs: "Iron is sharpened with iron, man is refined by his neighbor."

The conclusion of *Against Those Who Lead Astray* is also as combative:

> If someone wishes to contradict this work, may he not go and babble in front of children; better that he write a book and publish it so that competent people can judge what is true and refute what is false based on the authority of the truth.

It is especially in *The Unity of the Intellect* (*De unitate intellectus contra Averroistas*), which we will speak about shortly, that the harvest of these traits of impatience is at its most abundant. This can be explained, in part, by the heat of the discussion and the crucial character of the subject. It is in this book that Averroës is characterized as a "corrupter" and even a "perverter" of Aristotle's thought—though at least his intelligence is not in question. On the other hand, Thomas strongly doubts the intelligence of his Parisian interlocutors, whom he rudely writes: "Those who defend this position must confess that they understand absolutely nothing and that they are not even worthy to debate with those whom they attack." We can skip over other passages of this type in order to come to the conclusion, which is justly famous:

> with false knowledge, pretending to argue against what I have just written, let him not hide in a corner or speak in front of children incapable of judging such a difficult subject; let him write against this book—if he dares. He will have to deal not only with me, who is the least of them all, but with a crowd of

other lovers of truth who will know how to resist his errors and come to the aid of his ignorance.

I think we can agree that such polemics are not Thomas's best moments. We must remember that the man who writes in this tone is not a timid intellectual. He knows his worth and is not afraid to confront his adversary. At most, he perhaps regrets deep down that he has not found his equal. We can also see Thomas's deep sensitivity, which he struggles to contain so that his words do not wound too often.

An analysis of his handwriting runs in the same direction. It is worth sharing the expressions that appear frequently in the austere and fascinating world of a competent graphologist. They are surprising but are based on hundreds of examples. Thomas is "tense and hurried"; he "wants to go faster"; "this patience," which he will need to write correctly, "he does not have." It is not because he was unaware that his handwriting was legendarily difficult and was often not understood by his own assistants that he was trying to be clearer. "In a hurry," "fatigued," "distracted," he left in his text "lapsus," "cacographies," and "confusion." In his efforts at writing, when a subject or a word escapes him and thus he rewrites the same paragraph three times, "it happens that he writes the contrary of what he thinks, he forgets words," he breaks the continuity of his sentences, and he does not always correct them. Since we cannot say everything, let us conclude:

> Saint Thomas is a man in a hurry. He struggles with the exigencies of writing. He continually experiences his own distractions and thus interrupts himself and goes back over what he writes. He struggles with composing his thoughts and how to express them. He pays attention to details and is yet insouciant about the consequences that induce him to push forward with his irresistible ideas [M. J. Gils].

We concede that this portrait hardly fits with that of the timeless thinker that we have made of him who formerly had been called the *Doctor Communis* or *Angelic Doctor*. We may ask whether, even if this portrait corresponds to reality, it has little to do with his thought, which, at least, is fixed forever? This is far from being universally true: the progress that we notice in Thomas in his successive rewritings of certain points of doctrine witnesses against it. We believe that it would be interesting to look into what his concerns were at the time of his death, indications of which we can discern in his writings. There is more to win than to lose in this kind of research.

Without going too far into the question of Thomas's intellectual evolution, it would be unworthy to show a lack of interest in the one whom we venerate as a saint, or to neglect too much the man that he was and the model of the Christian life that he embodied. There is without doubt a continuity between the man who writes in this fashion and the one who blithely challenges his adversaries or becomes irritated with their inconsistencies. For this reason, we admire all the more the virtuous mastery that must have reigned over the birth of his more polished works, in which we almost never see his temper flare up. *A contrario*, the moments of impatience that we see in his use of strong language witness eloquently that Thomas's tempered spontaneity, which everyone sees as a mark of his genius, was clearly the fruit of his growth in virtue.

BENESCRIPSISTI THOMA·

THE *SUMMA CONTRA GENTILES*

f there is one thing that stands out for those who are seeking to discover who Thomas Aquinas was, it is his amount of travel. We first find him in Naples, then Rome, on his first trip to Paris at the time of his studies, then in Cologne, where he had followed Master Albert, then once again in Paris as a professor from 1251/1252 to 1259, and now here he is on the road to Italy, where he has been called for new tasks. Several years later, we find him for a third time in Paris before he finishes his days in Naples, where he had spent his youth. It can be estimated that he traveled some ten thousand kilometers, most of the time on foot, for it was forbidden for the brothers to use a horse. In our time, when trains and planes have become so commonplace, we can only admire Thomas's physical feats and, what is more, the mobility of this man whom we often picture surrounded by his books, as well as the ease with which he was able to cross borders. Latin was a plus and made him feel at home wherever he was. He was a European before Europe existed as such.

At the beginning of June 1259, Thomas left Paris for Valenciennes, where the General Chapter of the Dominicans was being held. There he took part in the work of a commission to promote studies. This commission, composed of five members, all of whom were masters of theology from Paris and the intellectual elite of the Order, was called together by the master general of the Order, Humbert of Romans. Given his explicit aim, the commission drew up a series of recommendations that were included in the Acts of the Chapter. These recommendations certainly provide us with the important work of the commission and the ideal of the Order on the question of studies, behind which stands a novel situation. While the first generations of Dominicans were made up of individuals who had often already been trained and were thus qualified to take on the work of leadership and teaching immediately, the influx of vocations brought with it younger men who sometimes lacked the basics. This issue had to be addressed. A good part of Thomas's work is a response to this need. The clearest example of this is the *Summa theologiae*. We will return to this soon, but we must first speak about the *Summa contra Gentiles*, which he had written earlier.

Date and Purpose

After the Chapter of Valenciennes, Thomas probably returned to Paris at least for a while, but we do not know exactly the date of his departure for Italy. In all likelihood, he returned to Naples, his monastery of origin, where he had begun his Dominican life at a time of tumult. We also have no idea about the eventual assignment that he was to undertake once he arrived in Naples. The only thing certain about this period is that Thomas continued work on the *Summa contra Gentiles*, which he had begun writing in Paris. What allows us to assert this is that we still have the hand-written version of this book. The beginning is indeed written on the same parchment and with the same Parisian ink as another work written in Paris a few months earlier. The conclusion is obvious: the change of parchment dates from the time when Thomas left Paris for Italy. The importance of this change in writing material comes from the fact that, in addition to other clues, it allows historians to suggest a likely time period for the writing of the *Summa contra Gentiles*: from the summer of 1259 to 1264/1265. There is more to this than a simple change of date. It allows us to follow the evolution of Thomas's ideas and to situate his other works in relationship to the *Summa contra Gentiles*. Thomas himself refers to the *Summa contra Gentiles* in *The Reasons of the Faith*, in the *Compendium of Theology*, whose connection to the *Summa contra Gentiles* is clear and manifest, and in the *Commentary on Aristotle's "De anima"*, in which he refrains from a lengthy critique of Averroës, since he had already done so elsewhere. All of these works appeared soon after 1265.

If the dates for the writing are pretty clear, the purpose of this *Book of the Truth of the Catholic Faith against the Errors of the Gentiles* (according to its complete title referred to by the first words of the manuscript) is the subject of lively debate. Who are these "Gentiles" referred to in the title of this work? To make things simple: in the New Testament, the Gentiles were non-Jews; with respect to this work, they are non-Christians. A later tradition summarized a response that for a long time had been considered a settled matter: Thomas would have written this work at the request of Raymond de Penyafort, the master of the Order, who had asked his young confrere to write a book in which the missionaries in Muslim territories, still quite close to Spain, could find the intellectual tools necessary for their mission. And yet, looking more closely, it is clear that Thomas was not specifically targeting either Averroës or Muslims. His work is far-reaching, and he examines and critiques a number of erroneous positions (pagans, Muslims, Jews, and heretics). What he writes is not simply an apologetic: it is really more a work of theology by its purpose as well as by its method. This does not keep us from seeing a universal apostolic purpose and thus we can discern Thomas's original intuition: that of a book addressed to Christians who are called upon to make contact with non-Christians, written in order to prepare Christians not only to dialogue with non-Christians, but also to familiarize themselves with the latters' objections and difficulties and eventually to respond to them.

Invitation to Humility

As for the method and the outline of this work, Thomas explains this clearly in a beautiful text that we will reproduce in full and then comment on it, since it is not only a summary of his understanding of theology, but also where he tells us clearly that he is offering a personal work. It is a privileged place for anyone who desires to explore Thomas as a person and not simply his writings. After three years of regency, the young master, in full possession of his talent and perfectly conscious of what he wants to do, lays out his first synthesis:

> Drawing from God's mercy the boldness of taking over the office of a wise man—which moreover exceeds our

strength—we propose as our aim to show as best as we can the truth of the Catholic faith and to reject contrary errors. In the words of St. Hilary, *the principal task of my life, to which, in conscience, I am obligated before God, is that all of my words and all of my feelings speak of Him.*

This passage, often cited, and with good reason, is remarkable for its tone, which makes the *Summa contra Gentiles* much more than a course or a work of didactics; it is also a personal reflection. As for Thomas's conception of theology, we must examine this more carefully, for this text presents a constant that we find in one form or another each time Thomas speaks of this subject in other works. He ascribes two main tasks to the theologian, according to his heart, and he expresses at one and the same time a resolute confidence in the use of reason in theology and a clear consciousness of what one cannot ask of it. He continues:

Ascertaining the truth sometimes requires that we proceed by means of demonstrative reasons capable of convincing our adversary. Such reasons do not apply in all cases, since it happens that we must not have the purpose of convincing our adversary by argumentation, but rather to resolve the arguments he makes against the truth, since natural reason cannot go against the truth of the faith. This particular manner of convincing those who are opposed to such a truth is taken from the Scriptures and divinely confirmed by miracles. In fact, we believe that which is beyond human reason by means of God's revelation. With the aim of shedding light on this truth, we can nonetheless put forward certain plausible arguments where the faith of believers is able to be exercised or at rest without the intention of convincing our adversaries. In reality, the very insufficiency of these arguments even

confirms them in their error by leading them to think that
we approve of the truth of the faith by rather poor means.

We cannot imagine a stronger recommendation to theologians. Thomas does not have to construct a hypothetical
system that would substitute his way of viewing things with
the way that God does. The humble and real theologian desires
to remain a realist and to adhere as closely as he can to what is
revealed. Thomas does not forget that his work rests on Revelation. According to a fitting expression of the Fathers, the "economy", that is, the way in which God makes Himself known in
salvation history, is the only path toward "theology," that is, the
reflection on the mystery of God who is the Author of salvation
history.

The rest of the text is nothing more than the opposite side
of the coin of the same truth and a new invitation to modesty.
Of course, Thomas knows not only the force of reason but also
its limits, and he illustrates his words with a concrete example:

> Pretending to prove the Trinity by means of natural reason,
> is to do wrong to faith in two ways.... First, by misunder-
> standing the dignity of the faith itself, which has as its object
> invisible things that are beyond human reason.... Then, by
> compromising the means to bring certain men to the faith. In
> fact to bring to the faith as proofs that which are not proofs
> is to expose the faith to the disdain of infidels, for they think
> that it is these reasons on which we rest our case, i.e., because
> of them that we believe.

With this background, which we must constantly keep present in our minds—for, in spite of appearances, Thomas never
forgets it—he can explain more deeply what he wishes to do in
the *Summa contra Gentiles*:

Our plan, therefore, is to proceed according to the proposed method. We will try to show this truth that the faith professes and that reason discovers by laying out demonstrative arguments and probable arguments, of which some will be by way of the works of philosophy and the saints (the Fathers of the Church), and which will serve to confirm the truth and to convince the adversary. After this, and moving from what is most clear to the least clear, we will present this truth that is beyond reason by refuting the arguments of the adversaries and by shedding light on, to the extent that God allows it, the truth of the faith by probable arguments and by virtue of authority.

Now that Thomas has presented his method, he can now sketch out the outline of his first three books:

We propose to follow the way reason and what human reason can discover about God. To this end, we will study that which is proper to God in Himself. Then, we will study the coming forth of creatures from God. Third, we will discover the ordering of creatures to God and their end.

These last words outline the structure of the first three books consecrated to truths accessible by reason. In more familiar terms, we can say: (1) The existence of God and the divine perfections; (2) the creative act in itself and all that makes up the universe, of which God is the origin; (3) the creature's return to God under the care of divine providence.

This draft still does not speak of Christ or the Trinity. Thomas reserves this for the fourth book of his work: the explanation of the truth of the faith that is outside human reason. Here there is nothing but *probable* reasons (relative) and no longer *necessary* ones (constraining), but Thomas does not hesitate to say something of the mystery. As he explains elsewhere, there are two types of theological arguments: one is to repudiate errors, and the other is to make truth intelligible. If one is happy with the first, the listener will undoubtedly know what is true and what is false, but will have no idea regarding the meaning of the truth that is presented to him. He will leave with his head empty. Like Montaigne after him, Thomas prefers a well-made head to a head filled with nothing.

Our Knowledge of God

It would be presumptuous to give even an approximation of the content of such a rich work in a few lines. We will have to settle for a few words on two rather general topics as an introduction to Thomas's thought: on the one hand, our knowledge of God, and on the other, his teaching on humans, which is to say, anthropology.

First, the treatise on God: After the "discourse of method" that we have just reviewed, the first book follows immediately on the existence of God. As it is not evident to us by itself, the existence of God must first be established, since it is "the necessary foundation of the entire work.... If this has not been achieved, then any study of divine realities will inevitably fall apart." And yet, to prove the existence of God is not enough. Thomas appeals very quickly to the role played by what is called the *via negativa* in his argumentation: by the *via positiva*, he says, we arrive only at the *existence* of God. When it is a question of His *substance*, this path proves to be inadequate:

> The divine substance, in fact, surpasses by its immensity all
> of the forms that our intelligence can grasp, and thus we
> cannot grasp it by knowing that it is. We still have a certain
> knowledge of it in studying *what it is not*. Because of our
> understanding, we are able to approach all the more this

knowledge, according to the extent to which we distance ourselves from the things of God.

We cannot underscore too much the importance of these sentences. For Thomas, it is not nothing to know about God then to know what He is not, for we thus distinguish Him from anything that does not belong to Him. In this way, from negation to negation, we arrive at a "true knowledge of the divine substance when God will be known as distinct from anything else. But there will be no perfect knowledge, for we will disregard what He is in Himself." The theological discourse in its entirety is, therefore, prefaced in the *Summa contra Gentiles* by the recognition of a certain impotency. Here, the experts use the word "apophatic": this word, which is Greek in origin (*apophèmi,* "to deny"), does nothing more than to summarize what we are trying to say. This approach to theology progresses from negation to negation, in such a way that even the affirmations—for there are some!—are laid out against the background of a "cloud of unknowing," in the words of the mystics. This acknowledgement of the inaccessibility of God is found more or less present at the end of the life of the author; in fact, it will never cease accompanying his work. And we discover it in the *Summa theologiae* as well as in his commentary on the *Sentences.*

Readers familiar with the history of medieval thought will think perhaps what Thomas owes to Maïmonides (1138–1204) and to his *Guide of the Perplexed.* This Jewish thinker's acute sense of the divine transcendence led him to bring to the fore of his thought the path of negation and the negative attributes, in such a way that he maintained to know nothing of "what God is," but only "that He is"—and this, moreover, on the condition of conceiving this divine existence in way completely other than that of our own existence. But we should not deceive ourselves.

Thomas goes much further than Maïmonides. Indeed, it is not enough to say that God is not a lion or a rock (to use biblical terms), if we must imply that He is a man. Moreover, we cannot say either that God is not a living being or that He is not good in the same way that we are if we are required to hold that our being or our goodness has no relationship to God. Goodness is but one example among other divine perfections; in any case, we must begin by distinguishing between the designated perfection and the way in which it is present in God. We can then say something like this to start: God is not good as a man is good; rather, He is the cause of everyone's goodness and of that of the entire universe. He is sovereignly good. Nonetheless, if we remain content with this, we risk limiting God to the same kind of goodness as ours. The *via negativa* has not lost its power, and there remains for us another step to climb: God is not good in the same way that we are good. Rather, He is good in a way that is unknown to us. This sums up what we mean when speaking about an analogical knowledge of God. Thomas has thus provided us with the means to speak about God in an effective way—allowing him to reach and to say truthfully something about God—but to remain respectful of His mystery—since the manner proper to the divine under which is achieved the perfection signified definitively escapes us. According to the teaching of the Fourth Lateran Council (1215), which Thomas certainly knew: "between God and the creature, we cannot emphasize a certain resemblance without the dissemblance being even greater still."

From this basic assertion, now firmly established and clear, Thomas can then enumerate all of the divine perfections as if he were not overlooking any of them, and he can maintain that God is sovereignly perfect and yet the object of knowledge and an "analogical" designation while keeping in mind the differences that apply. The theologian can really speak of God—without which he would have nothing else to do but to remain silent. This discourse is possible only on the basis of that which God Himself holds out to us by Revelation, but it is possible. And it is precisely here where Thomas differs radically from Maïmonides. Thus, when we say of God, as Jesus did, that He is Father, we know well that He is not our father in the same way that He is the Father of the Word. We cannot place divine paternity and human paternity under the same category. Still, He is truly father and it is from Him that all fatherhood takes its name.

The Divine Government and Humans

Since we cannot say everything, let us move on to the second part we wish to examine: the doctrine of man. In Book III of the *Contra Gentiles*, Thomas reveals his thought on providence and divine government; in other words, on the way in which God cares for this universe that He created and whose governance leads us to Himself. Without leaving God behind, Thomas proposes to focus his attention on humans, His creatures. In a direct line with what precedes, Thomas is not content with stating that God is good and that He is the cause of all the goodness of the beings He has created. Rather, he wishes to develop the implications of this fundamental view. Some are obvious: thus, in the name of the doctrine of transcendentals already discussed on the first page of the *Questions on Truth*, we grasp at first glance that if the creature is by definition a created being, it also has its own truth, its goodness, its beauty, and so forth, according to its degree of being. This general observation, already true in the absolute from all eternity in God, Thomas wishes to expand to the reality that we know.

In other words, with the government of the world, we leave behind the level of the divine eternity, in which is found the providence by which God leads all things to their end, no matter what happens, in order to enter into the time of the concrete realization of the design of providence. In the language of Thomas, it is the passage from the divine *thought* (Thomas uses the word *ratio*) of the ordering of all things towards their end to the *execution* of this ordering with all of the vicissitudes that affect the course of this world. While providence touches absolutely all beings in an immediate way, the divine government itself acts by means of diverse intermediaries, which includes you and me, on occasion. Nonetheless, this remains part of the general ordering of providence, for God never ceases being always present to all things that have life from Him, both in movement and in being. It is always He who gives to beings not only the capacity to be good as He Himself is good, but also to be in their turn the cause of goodness for other beings, which will be at their level, for themselves and for others, as so many particular realizations of providence. It is there that we discover the place of humans in the universe.

Thomas highlights one feature of the basic goodness of things, namely, the theme of the likeness of the effect to its cause. We will restrict ourselves to this. Even before coming to the specifically theological theme of man as the image of God, it is already true to say, on the natural level, that the creature resembles God in a twofold sense: not only "[is the creature] good as God Himself is good," but also "[the creature] moves another creature towards the good since God Himself is the cause of the goodness in others." It is under this dual aspect from which comes the double effect of God's governance over creation: the preservation of things in their goodness and their motion toward the good.

This teaching is nowhere better developed nor with as much insistence as in Book III of the *Summa contra Gentiles*. What is at stake appears in all of its clarity in the comparison of the position of certain Muslim theologians, according to whom, "no creature would have its own proper activity in the effects seen in nature: thus fire would not give warmth, it is God who causes the heat in the presence of fire and so on for all manner of natural effects." In favor of this strange position, they put forth a series of reasons that lead them to conclude the inefficacy proper to all human action, to the real inexistence of all inferior causes, in such a way, and definitively, that God would truly be the only One acting in all apparent causes of this world. We are speaking here of occasionalism: God would grasp only the occasion of our thoughts, gestures, or movements in order to produce the corresponding effect. We could speak also of fatalism: it is written.

Thomas has no difficulty in formulating the immediate objections that good sense opposes to this curious theory:

> In the hypothesis of the absolute powerlessness of creatures, it is God who would produce the immediate effect and, therefore, God's use of creatures in the production of effects would be useless.

This hardly resembles the idea that we have of divine Wisdom, and we know from elsewhere that "if God communicated to creatures His resemblance in beings by giving them being in return, He also gave them His resemblance in their actions in such a way that creatures themselves possess their own activity." This is not all. Brother Thomas ably demonstrates that this doctrine, which pretends to exalt God by reserving to Him the efficiency of all causality, ends, in fact, by showing Him a lack of respect by making Him little more than an idea of Him:

The perfection of an effect is the sign of the perfection of its cause; the stronger the force, the more perfect is its effect. Now, God is the most perfect of agents. Thus it is that He gives perfection to the beings He creates. *Therefore, to take away anything whatsoever from the perfection of His creatures is to remove something of the perfection of the divine power.* Now, in the hypothesis of the inefficacy of every creature, the perfection of the created world would be greatly diminished, since it is for a being the fullness of its perfection to be able to communicate to another its own perfection. *This position thus undermines the divine power* [Thomas develops still more arguments against this theory, arriving at similar conclusions]: God communicates His goodness to creatures in such a way that what one receives can be transmitted to others. *To refuse creatures their own action would be to undermine the divine goodness.*

We should especially notice the italicized words. Three times in the space of a few lines, Thomas repeats that to diminish the creature is to wrong the Creator. For Thomas, it is not a question of exalting God to the detriment of humans. In opposition to a spirituality in which the creature would be but nothing and in which humans should annihilate themselves so that God might be glorified, Thomas is convinced that God's greatness is affirmed in the greatness of human beings.

BENESCRIPSISTI THOMA

SOJOURN IN ORVIETO, 1261–1265

E
ven if we admit that that Thomas enjoyed several months of relative freedom for writing the *Summa contra Gentiles*, we should not conclude that he did not have other obligations. Quite the contrary. From September 14, 1261, he was named "reader" at the monastery in Orvieto, a small village north of Rome where the Pontifical Curia was staying. This position of reader had to be exercised in each Dominican monastery in order to ensure what we would call today the permanent formation of the brothers, as legislated at the General Chapter of Valenciennes two years earlier. Thomas thus had to provide a regular teaching schedule for those brothers who had not studied at the universities such as Bologna or Paris—which was the case for nine out of ten

brothers—in order to prepare them as best he could for the two main missions of the Dominicans, confided to them by Pope Honorius III: preaching and confessions "for the salvation of souls," in the words of the Dominican constitutions. Thomas's first task, then, was to form his brothers in pastoral ministry. He also had to ensure that there was a daily teaching on the Bible. For this work, he chose the *Book of Job*.

COMMENTARY ON THE BOOK OF JOB

One of the major themes of this book, and therefore of the commentary, is the mystery of providence. Thomas is very clear on this subject: "The whole purpose of the book is to show by probable reason that human matters are governed by divine providence." Now, this is also the subject of Book III of the *Summa contra Gentiles*, which was written at approximately the same time. It makes sense that Thomas had chosen to comment on the *Book of Job* so as not to break up his reflections too much.

To entice one to read Thomas's *Commentary on Job*, we affirm that it is one of the most beautiful scriptural commentaries that he has left us. Nevertheless, it is good to be alerted to the Scholastic and theological character of the commentary. We should not demand of his commentary what we are looking for in modern authors, not even the immediate spiritual applications provided to his readers, as Gregory the Great had offered to his readers in his own commentary 650 years earlier. Thomas states this explicitly in the introduction. In his commentary, Gregory essentially sees in the *Book of Job* an exhortation to patience in the face of adversity; he has only one purpose, a moral one. Thomas, for his part, turns the story of Job into a discussion on the metaphysical question of divine providence. If the suffering of the just is to pose a problem, one has to agree first of all on the fact that there is a divine government of natural things. That the just are afflicted without cause goes against the idea of providence.

One of the most original features of the Thomas's commentary consists in the way that he explains Job's words, even the most excessive ones. Thomas recognizes the road taken by the just. From the heartbreak of his losses, Job moves on to a rational discussion with his friends, before finishing by ceding to the divine inspiration and adhering totally to God's design, though without God's ever violating Job's freedom. It is still the same man from one end to another of the process, a man whose human and religious evolution we come to understand better.

Like the biblical book itself, Thomas's commentary offers a reflection on the most fundamental questions that humans face, since the tragic reality of the suffering of the just and innocent person is enough to inspire doubts about the existence of a divine justice, if there is no future world in which the good and evil will be rewarded or punished. Beyond a philosophical and theological anthropology that is found in Thomas's text, his book is presented as a meditation on the human condition.

Summary of Theology

Among the works that go back to Thomas's stay in Orvieto, *Summary of Theology* (*Compendium theologiae*), written at the behest of Raynald, Thomas's secretary and faithful companion, holds a special place. The similarity of this book with certain chapters of *Summa contra Gentiles* is so striking that one must conclude either emendations written shortly after this last book, or more probably parallel emendations done in the years 1261–1265. Taken up with other responsibilities, Thomas will not be able to finish the *Summary*. Improperly classified among the "opuscules," this work is without doubt one of the least known. Yet, we find in it a Thomas that we are not used to encountering, one who is concerned about simplicity and brevity, and one who deals with his subject in chapters that are generally rather short.

Careful to write a "summary", Thomas could not ignore the *Enchiridion* of Saint Augustine, who pursued the same end as Thomas, and it is undoubtedly from Augustine that Thomas borrowed the idea of constructing his work on the trilogy of the theological virtues. Like Augustine again, Thomas develops that which concerns the faith in relationship to the articles of the *Credo*, and what touches on hope in the demands of the Lord's Prayer; the section on charity, which Thomas had not written, would have, in all likelihood, been based on the *Decalogue*. This threefold arrangement is not uncommon in Thomas. We find this structure in the *Articles of the Faith* (*De articulis fidei et ecclesiae sacramentis*), which also follows the order of the *Credo*; we find it as well in his three long series of sermons on the *Credo*, the *Pater*, and the *Ten Commandments*. Thomas's choice of structure captures one of the spontaneous directions of his pastoral theology.

In addition, there is a personal touch that we should not overlook, which undoubtedly adds to a spiritual portrait of Thomas. He has forever earned his spurs in the task of popularization by explicitly situating his brief words under the rubric of *kenosis* (emptying) of the divine Word, who lowered his immensity to the limits of our littleness, and has left us, in his brief "*Summa*," the entirety of doctrine from the books of the Bible.

The "brief word" is a well-known theme of the Christian tradition, announced by the Lord to the universe, which Thomas adopts from St. Paul. In fact, he goes on to say: man's salvation consists in three things: knowledge of the truth as found in the Creed; pursuit of just ends, which the Lord teaches us in the Lord's Prayer; and finally, "practice of justice," summarized, according to Jesus himself, in the one commandment of love (see Mt 22:35–40). St. Paul means the same thing in his teaching that perfection in this life consists in observing "the three things that last: faith, hope, and love" (1 Cor 13:13).

It is from this Pauline verse that Thomas's general outline can be traced; it can only follow the three virtues in their traditional order, "for love cannot be true if the true end is not first of all rooted in hope, and this cannot be possible without knowledge of the truth." Thus, Thomas can conclude, for the benefit of his addressee, in the following words:

> You must first of all have faith in order to know the truth, then hope in order to direct your desire to its true end, and finally charity by which your love will be completely set right.

The Golden Chain (*Catena aurea*)

Amid the intense literary output of this period, we must set aside a place for Thomas's commentary on the four gospels by a series of citations from the Fathers of the Church. Known under the name of *Catena aurea*, this work was undertaken by Thomas at the request of Pope Urban IV at the end of 1262 and the beginning of 1263. The speed with which he completed this work is surprising, since the volume on Matthew would be offered to the pope before his death on October 2, 1264. One can suppose that Thomas had already begun assembling it even before the pope had asked him; his work was also greatly made easier by the fact that he could use florilegia and that he had been helped by a team of secretaries. They did not have to be highly qualified to gather the needed texts according to the gospel verses, with Thomas taking care of the final form. In all likelihood, he worked on the other three gospels at the same time—producing a well-rounded work—since he finished not long after, in Rome, between 1265 and 1268.

This collection of patristic quotations is presented as a verse-by-verse continuous commentary of the whole of the four gospels, such that it seems to have been written by one author. In order to do this, Thomas not only used materials that he had at hand; he also had translated from the Greek those texts that were not available in Latin. This is indeed a great novelty of the work, but we must also note Thomas's concern to introduce each quotation by the name of its author. This is remarkable because few authors before him, with the exception of Bede the Venerable (673–735) and Rabanus Maurus (780–ca. 856), had taken care to identify their sources precisely.

Thomas is quite clear about his methodological presuppositions. In introducing the way he wants this work to be used, he explains the manner in which he proceeded and states that he used shortcuts and lengthy editing to avoid wordiness. He also inverted certain passages for reasons of continuity: he even pointed out the meaning of certain texts. Still, contrary to what one might fear, the faithfulness of this work to the originals has not been found to be substantially altered. Careful checking has allowed us to recognize that all of the quotations are literal: Thomas abbreviates without altering the words; he does this only twice for two passages, in which the anonymous author allows himself a too-favorable opinion of Arius (256–336). Thomas's critical sense permits him to distinguish carefully between authentic works and those that are not.

At first glance a seemingly simple compilation, this work is, in reality, of considerable importance: First, in the quantity and quality of the material he used, since Thomas shows his knowledge, remarkable for someone of his time, of the Greek Fathers of the Church by making known to the Latin readers texts that were unknown in the West before their appearance in the *Catena aurea*. The importance of this work can also be measured by the use made of it by Thomas himself and by others after him. The last chapters of his *Commentary on Saint John* will be a rewriting of the *Catena*, and we can easily ascertain the influence of this work on his preaching. The same thing obtains for his theology, in which we discover that his use of patristic texts dealing with Christology increased sevenfold from when he wrote the *Sentences* to when he wrote the *Summa*. This knowledge allows us to understand better why the *Catena* is seen not only as being a turning-point in the development of Thomas's thought, but also as having a great impact on Catholic theology in general, since it had a wide audience. The richness itself of this work makes of it "a mine for exegetes, theologians, and preachers" (C. Spicq). The one whom we willingly regard as the model of metaphysics and speculative theology also occupies a first-place seat in the history of positive theology and patristics.

The Office of Corpus Christi

It is again to this period in Orvieto that we can date the composition of the *Office of the Holy Sacrament* that Thomas wrote at the request, once again, of Urban IV. A comparison with his other works reveals that this was for Thomas a decisive moment in his spiritual evolution. Fittingly, he centered the celebration of this feast on the mystery of Christ, God and perfect man, entirely contained in the sacrament and who so penetrates it that we do not say: receive the body and blood of Christ, but rather: receive Christ. When we compare the *Office* to Thomas's *Commentary on the Sentences*, we can see a clear evolution in his thoughts on the real presence. It is a foretaste of what will become the definitive formulation of the *Summa*: Christ does not present himself to us; rather, it is us that he makes present to himself:

> To live with one's friends is that which is quite proper to friendship . . . , and this is why Christ promised us his bodily presence as a recompense. . . . Nevertheless, in the meantime He did not want to deprive us of this bodily presence during our pilgrimage; by the truth of his body and blood he joins us to himself in this sacrament. . . . Thus this sacrament is the sign of the great love and the comfort of our hope by virtue of this very intimate union with Christ.

Thomas's use of hope in the text is not by accident, for if the celebration of the sacrament is pregnant with the memorial of the Passion, it is also turned toward the fulfillment of the end of time, since it is the pledge of future glory. This move in Thomas's Eucharistic theology toward the final fulfillment, absent in his contemporaries, is a good expression of his spirituality, which is so deeply marked by waiting for the vision of God. We can also notice a new presence of the affective element of Eucharistic communion. The word "sweetness" keeps recurring in the readings for the *Office,* and later the *Summa theologiae* will underscore that even if venial sins or distractions do not impede a fruitful reception of the Eucharist, the one who communicates in this state will be deprived of the sweetness of a certain spiritual reflection. Situated against this background, the biographical accounts concerning Thomas's Eucharistic devotion no longer seem devoid of all credibility; without going as far as to guarantee the literalness of Thomas's words, this theology gives to his words a mark of believability that no longer has anything surprising about it.

Adoro te

It is in this light that we should reread, or, even better, pray, the Eucharistic hymn known by its first two words. While we lack the space to reproduce the entire hymn, here are some verses that point to what we have just said:

> I adore you with devotion, Truth hidden
> You who, under these forms, are truly hidden.

We are immediately struck by the direct tone of this text. Several times we see Thomas addressing Someone, and he does so in the first person: "I adore You . . . You who hide yourself . . ."; "To You my heart submits itself . . ."; It is in You alone that I believe . . . in You alone that I hope . . . You alone do I love"; "Grant me . . . purify me . . .". This hymn is, before all else, a prayer. Thomas turns to Christ and tells him of his love. He implores and beseeches Him, like the good thief on the cross. He expresses his deepest desire: to live always with him and to contemplate him face-to-face. Or again—and this is no less present—the theme of God's hiddenness is repeated four times and assures us, like Elijah and Moses before us: "Forgive us! Show us your glory."

This direct way of speaking can be explained by the character proper to the Eucharist. For Thomas, it is not merely a sacrament among others: the Eucharist is the crown and the perfection of the sacramental system. It not only transmits the efficacy of the Passion, as do all of the other sacraments, it contains substantially Christ himself in person: his body, his flesh and blood, as well as his divinity. This is why, as in the Eucharistic liturgy, Thomas does not simply say: "receive the body or blood of Christ," but rather "Christ" and even receiving "God." He spontaneously uses the same expression in another prayer: "O sacred banquet in which we receive Christ!" And thus, when

Thomas speaks of the Eucharist, he uses the same words as when he addresses the Lord, as we speak to someone who we love:

> Grant us always to live from You
> And always to savor Your sweetness.

Of course, Jesus' passion is not absent from this prayer, which is as theological as it is fervent: "O memorial of the Lord's death.... From whom one drop of blood can save the entire world from all sin." Thomas uses this expression several times, which bespeaks his deeply felt conviction and faith: by virtue of the dignity of Christ's person, the least of his sufferings (*minima passio*) would have infinite value, that which gives him the very person of the Word. The Lord's passion was more than sufficient to return all of humanity to the Father, from whom they had distanced themselves by sin. If Christ accepted even death, it was to show the superabundance of his love for us. The hope in the absolute fulfillment at the end of time is no less forcefully expressed:

> Jesus whom I now see veiled
> When will be accomplished that for which I thirst?
> In order to see You with face unveiled
> I would be blessed by the sight of Your glory.

This will be the last word. The hidden God will then be completely revealed.

You may have already noticed: three of the four works that we have just briefly presented share one thing in common. Apart from their content (they are quite different from each other), it is interesting to point out how they resemble each other: Thomas wrote them at the invitation of someone else. Either at a friendly or fraternal request, like that of his *socius*, Raynaud, for whom he wrote *Summary of Theology* (*Compendium theologiae*), or by an official request, like that of Urban IV, which ended with the *Catena aurea* and the *Office of the Holy Sacrament*, or again from Jean Verceil, the Master of the Order of Preachers, who consulted Thomas several times. These writings form a part of a long series of twenty-six works (out of a total of ninety) that began at the time that Thomas was a newly minted bachelor with *Being and Essence* and *Principles of Nature* for the brothers of Saint-Jacques who had asked him to write them.

At Orvieto, these requests were multiplied. They are an echo of the flattery due his skill, which the Master of Paris readily accepted. It suffices to recall their titles in order to understand the diversity of these sporadic publications: *Buying and Selling on Credit, Against the Errors of the Greeks, Reasons for the Faith, Exposition on the First and Second Decretal, the Articles of the Faith and the Sacraments of the Church.* One should not construe from our silence regarding these writings that they are without interest. Far from it! They are certainly surprising, but even their diversity requires a few additional remarks.

These diverse titles allow us to conjecture that his sojourn at Orvieto was also for Thomas a period rich in human contacts. If he was, without question, a lover of silence and study, we also know that he had friends among his confreres, and the proximity of the papal court brought with it a number of contacts. We can already guess at the circumstances which we previously discussed and historians have labored to classify surrounding the identity of those who knew him or managed to befriend him.

Then, if we take a retrospective look at this period in Thomas's life, we cannot help but be impressed with the speed at which he worked. In six years (since he had left Paris), he wrote the *Summa contra Gentiles,* the *Commentary on the Book of Job,* the *Summary* of *Theology*, a good part of the *Catena aurea*, and an entire series of opuscules that are hardly negligible.

These four major works hardly have need of praise, since one of them alone would have been sufficient to keep the author busy. The shorter writings we owe above all to Thomas's intellectual generosity. Some sense, no doubt, a certain haste, and Thomas does not hide that he sometimes finds them too much and he could do without them, but he never refused. Moreover, they have the additional advantage of showing a theologian at work in the world of his time, attentive to the issues that others ask him about, trying to answer them in the best way that he can. The solitude of his monastery was not an ivory tower in which Thomas could isolate himself. In spite of a heavy workload as a teacher and an author, Thomas never shirked his duties of intellectual charity, and this is surely an element of his holiness.

BENESCRIPSISTI THOMA·

SUMMA
THEOLOGIAE

On September 8, 1265, or in the following days, the Provincial Chapter held at Anagni enjoined Thomas, "for the remission of his sins," to go to Rome and to establish a *studium*, a center for the formation of young Dominicans chosen from different monasteries from the Province of Rome. Their motherhouses had to provide for their needs. Thomas would have complete authority over them and could send them back to their motherhouses if they proved to be unsatisfactory in their studies. A full member of the Chapter and well-positioned to know what had already been decided at the General Chapter of Valenciennes, Thomas may well have been at the origin of this initiative. The foundation of a house of studies in Rome seemed to be a real chance given to Thomas in order to remediate insufficiencies in the formation of the brothers and, if possible, to better them.

THE SUBJECT MATTER
AND DATE OF THE SUMMA THEOLOGIAE

The innovation that Thomas would try in Rome cannot really be understood unless we remember his work in Orvieto. At the same time as his commentaries on Scripture, Thomas was also tasked with forming his brothers in moral theology and the pastoral dimensions of hearing confessions. This was in addition to preaching, which had been entrusted to his Order. Many manuals already existed that Thomas could not ignore, but he also came to realize the partial and incomplete character of the formation that they provided to future Dominican preachers. There was no rhyme or reason to their organization; each one limited itself to presenting the different virtues or different sins one after the other. The same was true for the sacraments. No attempt was made to examine the concrete problems that were raised. Nor was there a concern to establish these teachings on a firm scriptural foundation. Moreover, the properly dogmatic formation of the great truths of the Christian faith were dangerously neglected. We are not forbidden to think that Thomas profited from this experience to dream of something else. We should read, therefore, what he was going to do in Rome as an attempt to establish the formation of the brothers on a new and wider base. Leaving aside the *Commentary on the Sentences* that he had already taught in Paris, Thomas begins writing the *Summa theologiae*. This work will fill an obvious void by giving moral theology the dogmatic foundation that had been missing. This context allows us to understand better the beginning of the

Summa and what it teaches. Often cited, these couple of lines are sometimes only half-understood:

> Because the doctor of Catholic truth ought not only to teach the proficient, but also to instruct beginners . . . , we purpose in this book to treat of whatever belongs to the Christian religion, in such a way as may tend to the instruction of beginners.

We have often asked ourselves about the intellectual gifts of these students to whom Thomas offered a manual of such exceptional quality. It is possible that Thomas had overestimated their capabilities; yet he thought less about the greatest or lesser intrinsic difficulty of the materials to be taught than about how to organize it in a body of teaching that offered to students, not simply a series of questions juxtaposed haphazardly, but rather an organic synthesis that allowed his students to grasp the internal connections and their intelligibility.

> We have noticed that students in this doctrine have often been hindered by what they have found written by other authors, either on account of the multiplication of useless questions, articles, and arguments, or because those things that are needful for them to know are not taught according to the order of the subject matter, but according to a plan required by the book of the argument on offer, or, too, because frequent repetition brought weariness and confusion to the minds of hearers.

With this new book, Thomas undertakes a project that will fill most of his life. We can ascertain this from the following dates. It is certain that Thomas wrote the *First Part (Prima pars)* in its entirety during the time he spent in Rome (until 1268), and that it was circulated in Italy even before his return to Paris. The *Second Part* of the *Summa* (*Secunda pars*) what not written until he was in Paris, between 1270 and 1271. As for the *Third Part* (*Tertia pars*), he probably started to write it in Paris at the end of winter (1271–1272), and continued it in Naples until December 6, 1273, after which he stopped writing. By that time, he had written up to the sacrament of penance. The rest, under the name of *Supplement*, was written by his disciples, based on his *Commentary on the Sentences*. Thus, Thomas would have carried the burden of this work for the last seven years of his life, in addition to the other occupations that he had. This is undoubtedly the clearest sign of the importance that he attached to it. The *Summa theologiae* today is still Thomas's most-used work, even among those who consult it only occasionally. And it is still able to generate articles and translations.

Overview of the Summa

Before examining more closely certain parts of the *Summa*, we think that a general overview is in order. First of all, it will be useful to distinguish an overview from its content. There are as many commentators who are in agreement about the content, as there are who disagree about the overall structure. Unanimity cannot be achieved based on the fact that Thomas divided his work into three major parts, the second of which is further divided into two parts. This first remark still structures even today the usual division of the *Summa* into four volumes. In order to have a more precise understanding of the content of these material divisions, let us review what Thomas wrote with a thoughtfulness that does not belong to him alone:

> Since the principle aim of this sacred teaching (*sacra doctrina*) is to pass down knowledge of God, we will first of all speak about God (*First Part*), then the movement of the rational creature towards God (*Second Part*), and finally of

Christ who, according to his humanity, is the way that leads to God (*Third Part*).

Here, then, is an overview of the whole at its most basic. Thomas will be more explicit at the beginning of each of the following parts, and rather than listing them here, I leave it to the interested reader to look them up. As we did for the *Summa contra Gentiles*, we prefer to draw attention to certain points that will make our approach to this work easier and could highlight certain original points.

As long as we are dealing with recognizing the existence of the major divisions and sections, all of the commentators agree; the differences occur as soon as it is a question of knowing if a particular division, which is so simple in appearance, is not, in fact, hiding another less evident idea, whose internal movement could be more enlightening for understanding Thomas's teachings. It is worth recalling the steps that will allow us to conclude with a satisfactory explanation.

We have already proposed that the *Summa* should be read in the light of a Neoplatonic schema (inspired by the third century Greco-Roman philosopher, Plotinus), of the "exit" and the "return" (*exitus* and *reditus*). The *First Part* deals with the emanation of things from God considered as their principle; the *Second Part* speaks about the return to God as to their ultimate end. These two parts are tightly connected in their unity, which is that of two inverse movements. The same is true of the Bible, in which all creatures emerge from the hand of God and return to Him according to His design, since He guides the history of creation; in the same way, theology envisages this same reality from the standpoint of God. It is not, therefore, the theologian who reconstructs the intelligibility of the history of salvation after the fact, "it is the order of salvation which structures theology" (M. Seckler).

This explanation, which has within it the power and the seduction of simplicity, has led to many criticisms. In particular, it has the disadvantage of not integrating, from the start, the *Third Part*. Christ seems to appear as "a piece added after the fact," while Thomas speaks only about one movement of the creature to God, a movement that passes through Christ and reaches its goal only through him. Moreover, on the one hand, the "exit" is not identified with the *First Part*, because the "return" begins even before the end of this part, since Thomas already speaks about some aspects of the "return" that is common to all creatures, before specifying in the *Second* and *Third Parts* that which concerns the human person. On the other hand, the "return" is not limited to the *Second Part* but also reaches into the *Third*, for it is about a "return by Christ." In fact, there is at the same time an overlap of the notion of "return" in the different parts of the *Summa* as well as a lack of clarity regarding this concept. Given these criticisms, some abandoned the "exit-return" schema, which does not seem to explain much.

According to another explanation (with which we agree), there is no reason to renounce the "exit-return" schema, but we must specify that it does not have to do with the "economic" part (according to the theological meaning of the word) of the *Summa*. Prior to this, Thomas sets up another significant division that reiterates purely and simply, based on the Fathers of the Church, the difference between "theology" and "economy." "Theology" corresponds to the beginning of the *First Part* (Questions 2–43), which discusses God in Himself; while the "economic" takes in the rest of the *Summa* (from Question 44 onward) and the entirety of the 393 questions must itself be understood according to the schema of "exit-return". In the second part of the *Prima Pars* (Questions 44–119), the dominant movement (though not the only one) is again that of "exit" (even if for certain creatures, for example, the angels, the "return" is already implied). As for the *Second* and the *Third Part*, they speak only of the "return," regarding what is specific to rational creatures, that is, to human beings as the image of God. This movement reaches its climax when man arrives at the perfect resemblance of God, achieving communion with God through the mediation of Christ, "who according to his humanity is for us the way that leads to God." This explanation, complete and nuanced, seems to correspond well with what Thomas did. All the same, we have to add that "before being Neoplatonist, [this schema] is simply Christian" (M.-V. Leroy). What is more, Thomas highlights this explicitly when he says, with the Apocalypse, that God is the Alpha and the Omega of all of creation (Rev 1:8; 22:13).

The Place for the Mystery
of the Incarnation

This foray into the outline of the *Summa* is not gratuitous. Quite the contrary. If there is a privileged place for grasping in a few words the whole of Thomas's synthesis, it will be found here. The explanatory value that Thomas attaches to his structuring of the *Summa* is confirmed by the frequency of its use is various works: from the *Sentences*, whose choice was already pretty clear, to the *Summa*, in which all of the prologues carry the more or less explicit marks of this choice, by way of the *Summa contra Gentiles*. In fact, this schema is present in all of theology that structures itself on the faith and the Credo: from God the creator to God who comes back in Christ in order to take men with him in his glory.

Thomas's thought is deeply imbued with this circular vision of the world. And this to such an extent that he does not hesitate to say that the "circular movement is the most perfect of all, since it produces a return to the origin. In order that the universe might reach its final perfection, it must return to its origin." Here, Thomas returns to the classical expression of the movement of conversion as it had been previously expressed by Plotinus and his disciples. When he came across Aristotle's well-known assertion "by their very nature all humans desire to know," Thomas explains that this is so because it is only by this means that they can return to their source, and it is in this that their perfection consists; this is why the circular movement is absolutely perfect. Humans are indeed alone capable of a "complete return" to their origin by knowing God, in whom is their happiness.

Clearly, none of this makes sense except in a Christian vision of humans and the world. This is why Thomas took the trouble, at the beginning of the development on the incarnation in Book III of the *Sentences*, to include a well-known biblical verse on the rivers which return to their sources: "The rivers return to the place from which they left in order to continue flowing" (Ecclesiastes 1:7, according to the Latin text). From this image of the eternal return, Thomas does not conclude, as the biblical author does, about the vanity of all things; on the contrary, he argues:

> It is the mystery of the incarnation that is signified by the return of rivers to their source. . . . These rivers are, in effect, the natural goods that God gave to creatures: being, life, intelligence . . . and the source from which they come is God. . . . While they find themselves dispersed through all creation, these goods are found together in man, for he is like the horizon, the limit where corporeal nature and spiritual nature come together; being in the middle, they participate in spiritual goods as well as in temporal goods. . . . This is why when human nature had been reunited to God by the mystery of

the incarnation, all of the rivers of natural goods go back to their source.

Placed as it is at the beginning of an entire book, this explanation is not there by mistake. Thus, when we come across it again in an abbreviated form, we can conclude that it expresses a choice that Thomas held dear:

> The whole of the divine work finds its completion in this: that man, the last of the creatures to be created, returns to his source by means of a circle when, by means of the incarnation, he finds himself united to the very source of things.

In Thomas's thought, the incarnation introduces no discontinuity in the schema of "exit-return"; on the contrary, it is only by the incarnation that this movement attains its end. If Thomas uses the Neoplatonic schema, he feels free enough from it to introduce the Word incarnate of the Christian faith, and with it, salvation history. This is clearly not at all the thought of Plotinus. God is transcendent certainly, but His creation does not result from a necessary outpouring of the divine substance (what we call "emanationism"); rather, it is a free act of love, the same as His coming into the world thus created.

Finally, Thomas returns thus to the well-known biblical theme that the end of time ("eschatology," from the Greek word meaning "last") corresponds to its beginnings (in technical terms: "protology"), for only the one who has mastery of the end had the mastery of the beginning. This intuition allows him to propose a means of showing the whole of theology, by virtue of which he can make room for the contingent truths of salvation history. For Thomas, theology is not a science of the necessary in the way that Aristotle conceived of it; rather, it is an organization of contingent givens received by revelation, by which the theologian struggles to find the organization in God's design. This leads him to proceed more often by means of arguments of suitability rather than those of necessity. In this way, he can give full place to salvation history. In fact, in the *Summa* we find large slices of biblical theology, such as the work of six days, the treatise of the Old Law, or the mysteries of the life of Christ, which had found no place in a too-deductive understanding of theology that, precisely because of his use of the "exit-return" schema, Thomas can integrate without difficulty.

HUMAN ACTION IN THE LIGHT OF HAPPINESS

The study of the various questions treated in the *Summa* takes place entirely within the core of the framework that we have just described. It would be useless simply to try to list them, so we have retained only one point that appears to us to reveal the author's inspiration and analysis. Rather than directly discussing the subject of God and the domain of faith, we will speak about humans. More precisely, we will speak about the manner in which Thomas introduces his consideration on the behavior of the human being and of man's return to God in the light of the end that God offers him. Certainly, all things in the universe return to God, but man has the privilege of being able to do so in a conscious and free way:

> Man, being made in the image of God—meaning, according to John of Damascus [676–approximately 749], that he is endowed with intelligence, a free will, and the power of autonomous action—we must now take up, after treating the Exemplary, God [in the *First Part* of the *Summa*], that which concerns His image, man, according to what he is, that is, the source of his own actions, because he possesses free will and the mastery of his actions. What we will first consider is the final end of human life; after that, we will have to ask about

that by which man arrives there and how he can turn away from it; for it is according to the end that we must arrive at an idea of that which brings us back to it.

This text is remarkable on many levels. First, it establishes the consideration of human acts in the very nature of man (what we too quickly call, rather insufficiently, "moral theology," or even simply "morality"). The image of God, endowed with intelligence and autonomy, man is presented not as another being, but truly as God's partner. This "according to what he is" is of a rare boldness; it makes man not the equal of God, but a free person and therefore responsible for his actions before the throne of God. At the same time, this obliges man to conduct himself in a way worthy of this quality. It is here that we should look for the foundation of moral obligation when it presents itself, and not on any one commandment.

Next, we have to say something about the appeal to the final end of the human act. If this is so, it is because each course of action taken by the human person is situated between two aspects of the end he pursues. At the beginning—for, in the order of the purpose, the end is first—one has to know it and to desire it in order to direct oneself to it; at the end—for in the facts, the final end is directed or achieved. If Thomas, from the start, talks about the ultimate end, it is because the human person, given his quality as the image of God, can have no other end but Him, that is, to resemble Him. Of course, this final end will not be achieved except with the help of grace and in following Christ, who came to show us the way to this end. This is why that the *Summa* interweaves, between the study of human action and the blessed life, its treatment of Christ, "the unique mediator between God and humanity," as well as that of the sacraments, which are the "means" left to the faithful to help us on our journey. It is hardly worth mentioning, but it is this that brings to Thomas's understanding of the Christian moral life its own distinct flavor and that distinguishes it from a purely rational morality, which he would have found in Aristotle or his other ancient sources. For if Thomas wants to study human acts, it is in order to know what those acts are that lead us to happiness and those that keep us from having access to it.

Finally, the last thing to notice about this text, in placing the consideration of the end at the point of departure, Thomas clearly distances himself from the then-current Scholastic doctrine, which came from Peter Lombard, the author of the *Sentences*. And he seems to agree with Aristotle, who also speaks about happiness in the first and last book of the *Nicomachean Ethics*, but he quickly dismisses it by eliminating successively all "that does not lead to happiness" (riches, honors, glory, health, pleasures . . .), in order to return to a consideration of the ultimate end sought by means of these provisional goods. This is what he calls beatitude. He describes it in the first five questions of the *Second Part* of the *Summa*. Thus the vague notion of a happiness that is more or less consciously pursued cedes its place to a clearly identified beatitude that can be found only in the contemplation of God, the only object that can make us happy. Thomas establishes that this, and only this, by a new series of successive eliminations, a veritable negative dialectic that begins by showing that the happiness proper to humans cannot be uncreated, but rather created; that it cannot be a substance, but an operation; not a sensible operation, but a spiritual one; not an act of the will, but of intelligence, and naturally by speculative reason, and not practical, since God is not something "to do."

We cannot say everything in a few sentences. Nonetheless, we must warn against some ambiguities. In spite of appearances, this position does not exclude the will (love) of heavenly happiness. Thomas specifies only the role love plays: it sets the intellect in motion towards the still-absent end, and it rejoices in that end once it has been attained. But the intellect remains the only faculty that seizes the spiritual end. If happiness in act is inseparable from knowledge and love, that by which man appropriates it in order to enjoy it remains an act of the intellective faculty.

This thesis is not, moreover, that a selfish person in search of happiness (what we call "eudaimonism"), which subordinates the end to the one who takes hold of it, since the supreme Good subordinates all of the other goods, most especially so because it is not an object; rather, first and foremost, the supreme Good is a person (a communion of three Persons for Thomas!), loved for itself with a totally disinterested love of friendship (charity). Thus, we move from a love of pleasure for the end which, when well-ordered, will be integrated in the virtue of hope, to a love whereby we love the Good more than ourselves and in which we discover not only the necessary disinterestedness for a moral attitude, but also, as we have just said, the very foundation of obligation.

This description of beatitude would be incomplete if we failed to mention the role that friendship plays in Thomas's thought. Friendship is the bond of communion in the Good that consecrates the meeting of virtuous persons and completes their happiness. Moreover, in defining charity as a "species," the most eminent of which is friendship, Thomas shows that true and perfect beatitude finds its fulfillment in the communion of divine happiness, shared by those who are vivified by this charity-friendship. Charity thus becomes the essence of Thomas's moral theology. The theologian revisits, through the lens of charity, Aristotle's important intuitions of ethics for humans as "political" animals and his theory of friendship as "that which is most necessary in order to live". This heritage, fully adopted in the moral teachings of Thomas, thereby gets an unsuspected universality from Aristotle, for the social character of man goes beyond the narrow horizons of the city (*polis*) and of its citizens properly so-called, to whom Thomas was directed, by the charity that gives its full value to human action, his morality effectively spreads out to all human communities without distinction.

～～～

It goes without saying that we have often referred to the *Summa* all through this little book. Before returning to this, it is important to warn of a misunderstanding. Seen at a distance, the writing of the *First Part* of the *Summa* seems to have taken up all of Thomas's energy and free time. It was, however, not his only occupation. He had also to give time to the students entrusted to him, and this meant if not daily, at least frequent, meetings regarding *Disputed Questions*. He was also busy with a certain number of other writings. The disputed questions on *The Power of God* (*De potentia*) and the *Questions On the Soul*, as well as *Spiritual Creatures*, are all precisely situated by the scholars at this time. To this, one should add the commentary on *The Divine Names* by the anonymous Dionysius (who was believed to be the Areopagite, Paul's convert from Athens; this is why we now say: Pseudo-Dionysius), and the three commentaries on Aristotle's treatise *Regarding the Soul*, which had already been published before 1268 (the date of Thomas's departure for Paris). We can overlook other short writings that are far from being of the same importance.

Thus, our description of these three years that Thomas had spent in Rome has come to an end. Sent there in the name of obedience ("for the remission of his sins"), not only did Thomas oversee the teaching of his brothers confided to his care, he also showed the seriousness with which he took to heart his role as educator and to what depth he reorganized what was needed. It is finally his care as educator to which we owe the *Summa theologiae*, which has immortalized his fame. Simultaneously, he remained available for other occasional work, and if it is not impossible to guess what work he was sometimes asked to do, one must also state that he honestly tried to satisfy those who asked something of him. Finally, he also threw himself, at the same time, into his work of writing his commentary on Aristotle, which would become a nonnegligible part of his activity, and this in the interest of fulfilling his principal profession as a servant of the truth. If we remember that he also preached, we must recognize that his extraordinary gifts did not remain unused; we can also perhaps understand a little bit better the state of exhaustion in which Thomas found himself less than ten years later.

BENESCRIPSISTI THOMA·

SECOND TIME TEACHING IN PARIS: DOCTRINAL CONFRONTATIONS, 1268–1272

We find Thomas in Paris again in the fall of 1268. Given his status as a religious who had taken the vow of obedience, we can be certain that this new change of venue, as the previous ones, had not been decided by Thomas alone. The question may be asked: What were the reasons that motivated his superiors to send him back to Paris? We have an embarrassment of riches when it comes to conjecturing about the reasons for this decision. Of course, they do not exclude each other, and it is not certain that the real reason is the obvious one. For some, the Averroist crisis, about which we will speak later, was the principal reason; others think that it was about an increase of unrest on the part of secular professors against the mendicants; another summarizes precisely the situation by adding an additional motive: on returning to Paris, Thomas had to fight against all three of these difficulties at the same time. He had to fight against the conservative-minded of the Faculty of Theology, who saw in Aristotle a threat to the Christian faith. On the opposite side, he had to oppose the Monopsychist (one intellect only) Averroists. And finally, he had to formulate an apologia on behalf of mendicant orders against the seculars who wanted to exclude them from teaching at the university (G. Verbeke).

It is also striking to note that, during the same year, 1268, Saint Bonaventure, speaking about certain errors that threatened the Christian faith, denounced a threefold danger: the eternity of the world, the *necessitas fatalis*—in other words, the determinism of the will by the stars—and the unicity of intellect for all people. This last error is the worst one, he adds, for it encapsulates the other two. We are, thus, very close to the errors that Thomas is going to challenge. Given all of the other work he had in progress, in spite of his capacity for work, his astonishing concentration, and his ability to dictate to three if not four secretaries at the same time (we will come back to this), this was more than he needed to keep himself and his team busy. For us, it is a new opportunity to notice to what extent his work, which is often considered to be timeless, had frequently, in fact, been dictated by certain circumstances. If we have no further need to spend time defending the mendicant orders, we must, however, examine three opuscules that left a profound impact on the intellectual history of this period.

The Eternity of the World

The question was not new. Saint Augustine had already considered as acceptable the notion of a world without a beginning. This idea surfaced again after the introduction of Aristotle's philosophy at the University of Paris during the first half of the thirteenth century, putting it in the foreground. Most of the theologians of the time, such as Bonaventure and his Franciscan disciples, declared that the eternity of the world was unthinkable and that it was easy to prove by very effective reasoning that the world had a beginning. In opposition to this, Thomas argued that only faith makes us hold that the world had a beginning and that it is impossible to prove the contrary. While this may be true, it did not impede him teaching the fundamental and permanent dependence of the world on God. Thomas would never abandon this position, and he would address it again with force at another time in *The Eternity of the World.*

The Eternity of the World is dated to 1270, when the controversy worsened before provisionally being settled by the bishop of Paris, Etienne Tempier, who condemned thirteen philosophical propositions on December 10, 1270. It seems that we can assemble a probable context by considering this work of Thomas's as a reply directed to the Franciscan, John Peckam. At the time of his inaugural lecture, given in the presence of other masters, including Thomas Aquinas, Peckam had passionately delivered a thesis that stood in opposition to Aquinas's regarding the eternity of the world. Out of respect for the master's candidate, Thomas kept silent. When exiting the ceremony, Thomas's outraged students urged him to intervene. Thus, the following day, during Peckam's "resumption," (*resumptio*) of the thesis presented the previous day, and in keeping with the statutes of the university, Thomas intervened calmly and firmly and demonstrated to his opponent the fragility of his position. He did not stop at this oral intervention but wrote his short book not long afterwards.

The late date of this opuscule allows us to arrange in chronological order all of the texts which Thomas writes on this subject. We can see that he did not always hold exactly the same position. First influenced by Maïmonides, who had responded vigorously to Aristotle's thesis that the world is eternal and without a beginning, Thomas believed that the Philosopher himself considered his position to be only probable. Not wishing to give more strength than that accorded by its author, Thomas contented himself to say that it was not possible to prove peremptorily the beginning or the non-beginning of the world. After commenting on Aristotle's *Physics* for his own personal use, Thomas discovered that Aristotle's thesis was much more forceful than he had thought. This new certitude finds expression in our opuscule: not only had the non-eternity of the world not been proven, not only can it not be demonstrated, but an eternally-created world is possible. Still, Thomas did not cease believing the Bible and the Christian faith that the world had had a beginning. He simply writes that this truth is accessible only by faith. From a strict point of reason, nothing impedes us of conceiving the existence of a world perpetually created and perpetually dependent on God.

At this point, we cannot enter into the subtleties at this high intellectual level placed at the service of arguments for or against. Nonetheless, for us this discussion is interesting even if it goes beyond its immediate content. Here, Thomas appears as an author who is capable of changing his positions as his knowledge grows. Even more interesting is the clear distinction that he makes between truths that can be reached by reason and those that are accessible only through faith. We have already seen this, and the warning that follows is always the same: trying to prove too much discredits us in the eyes of our interlocutors. Thomas said as much regarding the Trinity, and he repeats it in speaking about the eternity of the world:

> With such arguments, one contributes more in deriding the faith than in confirming it if one searches to prove the novelty of the world against philosophers.

If we want to know what the characteristics of the Thomistic synthesis are, here is one that we find everywhere and that is enough to distinguish his disciples from those who are not. One need not reflect too long in order to understand that Thomas's position rests on the conviction that the created world has its own coherence, which is given to it by God, and which God Himself respects (as, for example, our free will!). The theologian cannot ignore this. On the contrary, he must insist on it. According to a formula to which we will return, grace does not destroy nature, but perfects it.

The Unique Character of Substantial Form

As with *The Eternity of the World*, this new question is situated within a polemical context. In order to assist the reader to understand what this question is about, let us recall what is meant by "substantial form," and even more simply "form." According to Aristotle, who is at the origin of this phraseology, every being in this world (animate or inanimate) is composed of an inseparable bond between two complementary principles: matter and form. In technical terms, philosophers call this "hylomorphism," from two Greek words: *hylē*, matter, and *morphē*, form. It is enough to know this without going into details. In concrete terms, the human person is a unique and indivisible composite of two elements: matter, which is the body, and form, which is the soul. These two elements do not exist separately one from the other; we can only think of them in their mutual relationships and their complementarity. In our case, we refer to this as "substantial form" because the human person is a substance, a subsistent being of a rational nature. In this unique composite, it is easy to understand that the form is the principal element: but it would be nothing without the matter that it animates. It is the form that allows the individual to exist at all, and, at the same time, allows it to be what it is and to act accordingly. Because of fact that we have a human soul, we are capable of thinking and acting as rational human persons. Animals, too, have a soul, a soul that corresponds to their animal nature, according to which they act.

Since we are individuals composed of a body and a soul, there are in us different of levels of life, which vary as the soul and the body are more or less implicated (we eat and are nourished by our bodily organs, we perceive by virtue of the senses, we reflect by virtue of our intelligence). We speak about a vegetative life, a sensitive life, or an intellective life. Given this diversity, the question that we now ask is how to know if one and the same soul suffices to fulfill these different functions. In short, according to Thomas, the intellective soul is the only substantial form of the human composite, and it exercises this function at different levels of the composite life: vegetative, sensitive, and intellective. The human soul passes through the first two steps before arriving at its fullness with the third, but it never ceases exercising these functions. The soul, therefore, is the unique form of the body and it cannot not be other, for if the soul is the form of the composite human being, it is the soul that gives being and life, and there can be only one form for each individual. Thomas's adversaries, on the other hand, held to a plurality of forms according to the different levels at which life is seen.

We have spoken about Augustinianism in contrast to Aristotelianism, but that contrast is only partly true. It is true that we once again find Thomas and the same Franciscan adversaries face-to-face concerning the eternity of the world. But we cannot reduce things to this rivalry, for a good number of Dominicans were also opposed to Thomas on the same topics. Far from being new at this time, the problem had occupied minds for fifty years, and the greatest diversity ruled among the partisans of the plurality of forms, especially among those masters who were tainted with Neoplatonism. Moreover, if certain partisans of the plurality of forms also pretended to lay claim to be of the school of Aristotle, Thomas could claim to be an authentic descendant of Augustine as much as they were.

The violence of the confrontation can be explained especially by the conviction that the theses of Thomas on the unicity of the substantial form and on the eternity of the world posed a threat to the Christian faith. Regarding the eternity of the world, Thomas was not convinced and persevered in his position until the end. He did the same with respect to the unicity of the substantial form, but here the debate veered from the area of the theology of creation to that of the theology of human composition, anthropology, and, even more, the theology of Christ, that is, Christology.

Already heated, from the strictly philosophical perspective, the discussion became sharper when it became more theological. The focal point of the quarrel was one of those questions for which the Scholastics had a talent. It is revisited in various ways in the *Quodlibets* that Thomas had to defend during Advent and Lent of 1269–1270. One question—insignificant at first glance: "Are the preceding forms destroyed with the arrival of the intellective soul?" For Thomas, the response was negative, since the human soul combines the vegetative, sensitive, and intellective functions. This first question is followed by a series of apparently gratuitous others. "Did Christ remain man during his three days in the tomb?", or even, "Was Christ's eye after death really an eye or merely equivocally so?" Apparently far-fetched, from our vantage point, the question is still justified, since the organ, now deprived of life, is no longer what it had been.

We need to pause with a last question: "Did Christ's body remain numerically the same on the cross as in the tomb?" The insistence on returning to these questions shows the preoccupation of thinkers of this time which, for us, are gratuitous and futile, but in reality for them raise the most profound problems of Christology. According to his adversaries, Thomas's response to this last question is heretical because it calls into question the identity of the body of Christ before and after his death. Given that the soul is the unique form of the body, and Christ's body was momentarily deprived of the soul after his death, we can no longer say that the body in the tomb was the same as that of the living Christ. To avoid this consequence, Thomas's adversaries theorized the existence of, in addition to the intellective soul, a "corporal form" that, while remaining the same, remained attached to his body before and after death and could ensure the unity and continuity between the two states of Christ's body.

Thomas, like his adversaries, is not in doubt about the numeric identity of Christ's body before and after his death. Nevertheless, for him, it is not a corporal form that preserves it but rather what we call the "hypostatic union," that is, the union of Jesus' soul and body to his divinity in the one and same person (*hypostase*), the incarnate Word. A being remains numerically the same, Thomas explains, when there is the same subject, the same person, whatever it has gone through. Now it is well established that Christ's body, whether living or dead, has no other person than the Divine Word, since the union of the

Word both in Jesus' soul and in his body did not stop at Jesus' death. Jesus' body and soul have, therefore, maintained their relationship to the unique person of the Word, and it is this that preserved their numeric identity in spite of Jesus' death. There is thus no need to involve a hypothetical corporal form when we have the assurance of a quite certain dogmatic teaching, believed by the Christian faith since the fourth century, namely, the permanent union of the person of the Word in soul and body beyond death.

The Unity of the Intellect
in Opposition to the Averroists

Over and against the conservatives, Thomas also had to combat what—for reasons of convenience—was called "Averroism," named after Averroës (1126–1198, a Muslim from Andalusia, physician and philosopher, who wrote in Arabic), who played an important role in this new controversy by his interpretation of the Aristotelian theory of the intellect. In his condemnation of December 10, 1270, the Bishop of Paris, Etienne Tempier, had gathered thirteen propositions taken from some heterodox leanings that shook the University of Paris and that we can sum up under four principal points: the eternity of the world, the denial of the universal providence of God, the unicity of the intellective soul for all humans (or monopsychism), and determinism. The first two propositions sum up what Thomas wanted to say in his new treatise, *On the Unity of the Intellect, against the Averroists* (*De Unitate Intellectus, Contra Averroistas*): "The intellect of all humans is unique and the same for all"; "the expression 'humans think' is false and improper." The identity of the "Averroists," who hold these positions, gave rise to inquiries with sometimes contradictory results. We will pass over this. It will be enough to know that Averroës's representatives will be found especially among the philosophers (at the Faculty of Arts, as it was called at the time), and we place at their head the best known among them, Siger de Brabant, even if he was not the only one concerned.

Before we delve into *On The Unity of the Intellect*, it will be helpful to specify what we understand by this word intellect. Very briefly stated, the intellect (*intellectus*) is human intelligence as distinct from reason (*ratio*). In reality, these two words refer to the two functions of our intelligence: by intellect, we mean the intuitive capacity that allows us to "see" exterior realities, to strip them of their individual characteristics and to make of them so many intelligible objects, while, by reason, we are able to put together objects perceived this way, and to pass from one to another in a "discourse," a sort of discursive step, which allows us to reach a conclusion that is formulated by the intellect, as for example: such an effect universally comes from such a cause. More often than not, we do this without thinking about it, and each of the moments of the intellective knowledge deserves to be understood in more detail, but this is not our subject. We simply have to note that here Thomas does not reduce the intellect only to the factor of knowledge; it also encompasses the will, the desiring.

> This is obvious to anyone: in fact, take away from humans all diversity of the intellect—that which, alone of all parts of the soul, appears incorruptible and immortal—and it will follow that after death nothing will remain of human souls except the unique substance of the intellect alone; you will thus suppress the distribution of rewards and punishments until nothing distinguishes them. No, our position is to show that the aforementioned position is also contrary to the principles of philosophy as well as to the doctrines of the faith.

To address this issue, Thomas will proceed in two stages. Alain de Libera, an excellent scholar of Thomas's work, writes that Thomas's book is certainly a work of philosophical polemics, "it is also and foremost a lesson on reading and a lesson on history." In the first stage, the first two chapters, "philological", Thomas proceeds with a tight discussion of the texts, and, using the most recent translations of Aristotle and his commentators, he shows his adversaries to what extent their "Averroës" is simultaneously opposed to Aristotle's teaching "averrorised" and to the Christian faith. In the second stage, the three final "argumentative" chapters, he discusses the basic propositions.

> [By means of a profusion of closely woven arguments he succeeds in showing that if the intellect is that which is the principal in humans and if there is only one and the same intellect for all, it necessarily follows] that there would be no more than one thinker, no more than one who desires and no more than one user according to free will, of everything that distinguishes one human from others ... that there would be no difference between them regarding the free choice of the will and that it would be identical in all. What is clearly false is impossible. It is in fact contrary to all that we see, and this would destroy all moral science and all that would come from life in the human community, which is nevertheless natural to humans, as Aristotle said.

Thomas can thus challenge the "Averroists" to render an account of this given common experience: "That man thinks." These arguments seem to have embarrassed them, especially Siger, who had already read Thomas's *Sentences*, and was thus led to continue to reread his work and seems to have evolved, as a consequence, to less heterodox positions. No doubt, he continued to oppose his exegesis of Aristotle to that of Thomas, but he names Thomas and Albert as being the two thinkers who count the most in philosophy, and he concedes that, to understand, the intellect works interiorly in man. Going even further, he writes elsewhere: "The intellect is joined to the body by reason of its nature.... The intellective soul is the form and the perfection of the body." Thus, there is no longer question of an intellect separated from the body, unique for all humans.

It is hardly necessary to add that through all of these discussions, which sometimes take on the aspect of jousting matches of logicians in appearance far removed from reality, what safeguards Thomas is a certain vision of the human being. First of all, it is a realistic vision: the unity of the human composite, inseparable soul and body, was rather mishandled by "Averroist" theories. At the same time, Thomas's vision was Christian: Thomas was angry at the fact that Christian philosophers dared to uphold these theories, and he openly wondered if they truly understood what they were talking about. He uses the harshest words of his polemical wit against them. We will soon return to this vision of man and the role that it played in Thomas's synthesis.

These discussions, briefly reviewed here, are not purely of intellectual interest: they are also essential for grasping Thomas's personality. The biographical sources happily underscore his kindness and humility when faced with Peckam in spite of the latter's impetuosity—it is also true that Peckam himself spoke of Thomas's humility. Still, we cannot restrain ourselves from noting that in these controversies Thomas remains the same: as a wrestler who does not hesitate to fight when it is called for and who is ready to respond to any challenge; loyal and rigorous, for sure, also impatient in the polemics against his adversaries who do not understand the weight of an argument, indignant at their raising questions that weaken the faith, and even ironic when he addresses them by paraphrasing the *Book of Job*, as if they were the only reasonable human beings with whom wisdom would seem to have appeared.

More than these changes of mood, which do not show Thomas at his best, but which demonstrate in their own way the ardor of the controversy and no doubt the worry of a believer confronted with these challenges, we need to underscore once again his will not to compromise the faith—under the pretext of defending it—by a counterproductive argument. As it sometimes happens in a circle of theologians, where the faith is surreptitiously invoked in order to lend strength to an argument that, by itself, has none. Thomas thinks of the image that theology herself gives to the formidable dialecticians of the Faculty of Arts and, at the risk of making his job momentarily more difficult, he refuses to depreciate the requirements of reason.

Thus, he not only gives proof of intellectual loyalty; he commands the respect of his stubborn adversaries who will agree to dialogue with him, as was the case with Siger. He thinks, too, of the transcendence of God, which his apologists inadequately ridicule. This was not simply an attitude of the scholar or the professor; it was also that of the preacher concerned with the faith of believers. In the sermon "Watch Out for False Prophets," which nevertheless denounces "those who say that the world is eternal," he warns against those who raise objections that they cannot resolve, for they agree with their adversary: "To raise an objection and leave it without a solution is the same as conceding the argument."

BENE SCRIPSIS TI THOMA

SECOND TIME TEACHING IN PARIS: ON SAINT JOHN AND DIVERSE MATTERS

The motives for Thomas's return to Paris led us to speak in the first place about his engagement in contemporary controversies. It is important, however, to avoid a frequent error of perspective and to imagine that he was so embroiled in these matters that he gave all of his time to them. This is far from the truth! His primary occupation remained teaching the Bible, and it is to this period that we owe some of his most famous works, one of which is his *Commentary on Saint John.*

His Teachings on Saint John

His teachings *On Saint Matthew* occupied his time during 1268–1269. His teachings *On Saint John* in this second period in Paris took place in 1270–1271. There is nothing surprising about his transition from the first to the last gospel. What is clear is that Thomas took the books of the New Testament according to their canonical order. He went directly from Matthew to John, for Matthew took the place of two other gospels, Mark and Luke, which have many points of contact with Matthew, while John has something particular to say. Thomas is very clear in his Prologue: "The other evangelists deal principally with the mysteries of Christ's humanity; John, in his gospel, highlights in a special way Jesus' divinity.

These several words provide us with a precious framework for reading, for this same phrase reoccurs at the end of the book. In commenting on the appearance of the resurrected Jesus to the apostle Thomas, until then unbelieving, who cries out: "My Lord and my God" (John 20:26–29), Thomas explains what is happening with his patron saint: "In confessing the true faith, the apostle Thomas immediately became a good theologian, who recognizes Christ's humanity and his divinity." It is also no doubt for the same reason that, from the beginning, the apostle John is presented—according to the entire tradition—even as a type of the contemplative and that Thomas has a keen awareness of the insufficiency of theological discourse on Christ:

> The words and gestures of Christ are also the words and gestures of God. If someone wanted to write them or recount them in detail, he would not achieve it. What is more is that the entire world would not suffice. An infinity of human words cannot attain to the unique Word of God. We have written about Christ from the beginning of the Church. Yet, this is still not enough. Even if the world would last hundreds

of thousands of years, the books that could be written about him would not be enough to arrive perfectly at his gestures and his words.

Even if it would be a little fruitless to try to rank Thomas's best commentaries on Scripture, it is certain that we can classify this one, along with the *Commentary on Job* and the *Letter to the Romans*, among the most complete and the deepest that he has left us. Some have no fear of asserting that *On Saint John* "holds a unique place" and that one could even say that it is "the theological work par excellence of Saint Thomas." Such praise can be explained if we recall that the "*Gospel of John* contains what is the most ultimate in Revelation." We cannot recommend enough reading, in translation, the superb lessons on the mystery of the Incarnation found in the Prologue, or of those no-less-beautiful words concerning the Holy Spirit on the subject of "the wind that blows where it will," or "the source of living water that flows from his side" of Jesus on the cross, or, again, on the coming of the Paraclete, the Consoler, from chapter 14 to 16, which concludes Jesus' work and leads to the fullness of truth. In this commentary, Thomas reveals himself as being one of these contemplatives of whom Saint John is the type.

THE QUODLIBETAL DISPUTES

As for the ordinary disputations that Thomas started to hold again in the context of his university activities, we can count an annual average of thirty-five. This is a lot, but it is far less than the average of more than eighty annual disputations that were held on his *Questions on the Truth*. In keeping with what we have already seen during his time on Rome, the more-mature Thomas has clearly limited the frequency of these disputations in order to reserve a little bit more free time for his other tasks.

The various disputations or the Aristotelian commentaries were produced in tandem with Thomas's writing of the *Summa theologiae*. Without implying that there is a complete simultaneity between the elements of each one of these parallels, it does point to a temporal proximity. Brother Thomas was a formidable and rapid worker, but he was also careful to avoid dissipating his concentration and his strength. Without bringing this matter to a close, we have to mention at least the series of *Questions on Evil* and *On the Virtues*, as well as the *Question on the Union of the Incarnate Word*, which were produced more or less at the end of this period.

Since we already know the ordinary disputed questions, it will be good to pause a little on the quodlibetal disputes. This academic activity, which was so characteristic of the medieval university, has been the subject of many studies, and, perhaps without revealing all of its secrets, they are now well-known. It took place two times per year during Advent and Lent and lasted for two sessions. In the first, and as the name indicates, the attendees, be they masters, students, or the simply curious, could raise all sorts of questions (*de quo libet*: regarding what one wants). The master normally let his bachelor respond, and he intervened only if his second was in difficulty: the master reserved it for himself to give his magisterial determination in the second session, which took place either the following day, or several days later.

This activity [the magisterial determination], reserved to the masters, was nevertheless not an obligation. If it is an exaggeration to say that only the masters dared to engage in this perilous exercise, it is also true that not everyone participated, and it is also noteworthy that some even took pleasure in it and turned it into a privileged form of expression. The uncontested champion was Gerard d'Abbeville, a secular master, a rival of

Thomas Aquinas, of whom we have already spoken, and from whom we have twenty quodlibets, while Thomas had held only twelve. If, as we can gather from reading the lists of proposed subjects, the freedom of expression was not simply empty words, the exercise was nevertheless not one of pure spontaneity. The master himself could propose certain questions and impel colleagues, bachelors or students, to respond. If it were also possible for him to decline to answer a particular question that he thought was frivolous or out of place, he was certain that too many refusals would have hurt his reputation. If the universality of the subjects treated was real, it was nevertheless not about "whatever." We have been able to determine that 90 percent of Thomas's quodlibetal articles had their parallels in other places in his corpus. This is a way of highlighting that only those subjects deemed worthy of a master were retained.

Given its style, the quodlibetal literature is strongly rooted in what was actually happening at the university, for instance, the unicity and plurality of forms. We also find more down-to-earth questions that hint at the immediate worries of those present. Made up mostly of clerics, this public made clear their pastoral concerns regarding matters of private, social, and economic morality. These concerns, along with those of the University, represent the entire life of an era, which we can see in the quodlibetal literature, and it is this that makes them a fascinating subject of study.

Without enumerating all of the subjects dealt with by Thomas in these public discussions, and thus without the risk of tiring the reader (there were 264 subjects in total, which means an average of 20 for each session), it is interesting to gather what they teach us about their author. Even carefully reviewed by Thomas, these texts have retained some echo of the discussion from which they came, and some of them are very clear concerning the awareness that Thomas had of himself as a master of theology. It is worth the effort to return to the quodlibet of Easter 1269, in which he examines the question whether it is a waste of time to give oneself to studies or to teaching.

Thomas examines things from a high level and compares his work to the construction of a building for which one needs architects and manual laborers; the former exercise a more noble task than the latter and receive a better salary as a consequence. The same thing obtains in the construction of a spiritual edifice, which is the Church:

> There are those that we can compare to manual laborers whose task is to take care of individual souls, e.g., by administering the sacraments and other similar tasks. Those who are compared to architects are the bishops who oversee the work of the former and make it clear how they are to carry out their work; this is why, for instance, we call them "*episcopes*," or "superintendents." Similarly, doctors of theology are also architects who research and teach how the others must work for the salvation of souls.

> To speak absolutely it is better to teach theology—and more meritorious, if it is done with a good intention—than to give oneself to the individual care of this one or that one. This is why the Apostle says of himself: Christ did not send me to baptize but to preach (I Corinthians 1: 17), even though to baptize is more apt for the salvation of souls. Saint Paul says again: "... entrust to faithful men who will be able to teach others also" (2 Timothy 2:2). Reason itself shows that it is more profitable to give instruction on the knowledge of salvation to those who can make progress both in themselves and in others than to instruct the simple who alone are capable of benefitting from it. Still, in the case of imminent necessity, bishops and doctors should leave behind their own

office in order to give themselves to the salvation of individual souls.

This text, strongly inspired by Aristotle, has no doubt something a little astonishing about it to a reader of the twenty-first century, who runs the risk of being shocked by this manner of considering the pastors of souls as simple spiritual "manual" laborers while the theologian raises himself to the level of an aristocrat like a master builder. The hearers of these words would have been just as surprised: this text does not only translate the high social position of the masters of the University of Paris (they were hardly a handful for all of Christianity), it also expresses the complementarity of tasks in the body of the Church. The theologian defines the general principles; concrete pastoral service concerns itself with individual cases. As for the rest, fulfilling the necessity of getting one's hands dirty if the need presents itself, reorders without saying as such the true hierarchy of values.

Separate Substances

The public activities of polemics or teaching must not hide the intense personal work that the master of Saint-Jacques continued to complete. It was during the years 1268–1272 in which Thomas wrote the enormous *Second Part of the Summa theologiae* (between January 1271 and Easter 1272) and when he begins the writing of the *Third Part*. He also did not stop responding to occasional requests that his intellectual charity called for and that, at times, tried his patience. As was the case at Orvieto and at Rome, this last stay in Paris also found him involved in individual consultations that Thomas could not avoid. We have already mentioned several to which we must add others. He also wrote other significant works.

The short book *Separate Substances* is a response to a friendly request, and even though Thomas never finished it, it still has twenty chapters, which adds up to forty or so pages in the great Leonine edition. The author expressed himself clearly regarding his plan right at the start of the Prologue: he wants to speak first of all about the holy angels and to recall, in the form of a conjecture, what the thinkers of Antiquity thought of it. If he finds something that is in conformity with the faith, he will use it to his advantage and he will refute what is contrary to Catholic teaching. These two steps are very clearly marked at the beginning of Chapter 18:

> Since we have seen what the main philosophers, Plato and Aristotle, thought about the subject of spiritual substances, of their origin, of the creation of their nature, of their distinction, and the manner by which they are governed, we must now show what the teaching of the Christian faith says about them. To this end, we will especially make use of the works of Denys, who dealt with spiritual substances better than all of the others.

Thomas scarcely began the second part of his work, since he stopped after twenty chapters—right in the middle of his development on the sin of the angel, which he had just said presents a lot of difficulties. The importance of this treatise is not measured by how thick it is: we could speak of it as "one of the most important metaphysical writings of Aquinas," while others consider what was said about Plato in the first chapter as the most elaborate Platonic synthesis that we can find in Thomas.

The Commentary
on the Book "About Causes"

Even though this commentary was not, like others, written at
the request of someone else, there is still good reason to speak
about it here, because of its probable date (the first half of 1272)
and especially because of its relationship with *Separate Substances*. Even today, the author of the book *About Causes* (*De
causis*) is not known with certainty; however, because [Thomas
had encountered] the translation of *Elements of Theology*, which
had been written by Proclus—who, in the fifth century, was
thought to be one of the last successors of Plato at the Academy
of Athens—Thomas was the first to identify *About Causes* as
coming from an Arabic philosopher who had borrowed heavily
from Proclus's work.

For Thomas, commenting on this text was thus for him a
means of pursuing a dialogue with Neoplatonic philosophy,
which had already been clearly tempered by the author of
the book *About Causes* in the direction of monotheism and
a moderate realism. An excellent scholar put it well when he
commented on this text that Thomas has three books opened
in front of him: "the text of the *Liber*, a manuscript of the *Ele-
mentatio* and some Dionysian writings. The texts of these three
authors are cited *ad litteram*, while the other others used, principally Aristotle, are cited *ad mentem*" (H.-D. Daffrey). There
we can find the particular interest of this undertaking: "The real
intention of Saint Thomas in this *Commentary* is to compare the
three texts. The entire argument of this work is here, and it is,
perhaps, a unique case in Thomas's work." Thus, he will be able
to give to each its rightful place and to situate himself against
Proclus, on one side, and, on the other hand, with the author of
the *Liber* and with Denys "of whom he underscores the similar-
ities between Aristotle or Saint Augustine." This is why Thomas

refuses the notion of separated forms and divine substances, the polytheism of Neoplatonism, its "emanantism" also (we recall that one designates the flow of beings from the divinity), and the priority of the one and the good of being, "but he carefully keeps as part of his synthesis the major orders of creation: being, living, intelligence, and God over everything."

In order to make a complete review, let us recall that in Paris, as previously in Orvieto and Rome, Thomas's knowledge had been sought on several subjects that are sometimes surprising to us: *The Mixing of Elements*, *The Movement of the Heart*, *The Hidden Workings of Nature*, *The Judgment of Stars*, *Random Drawing*, *The Secret of Confession*, *The Letter to the Countess of Flanders* (often improperly referred to under the title *The Government of Jews*). This dry listing, to which we are constrained by the limits of this book, should not lead us to believe that these short works lack interest. On the contrary, each one of them carries the signature of its author: what is surprising is their diversity. Knowing his title of "Master of Sacred Scripture," we more or less expect that Thomas is a man of one book, the Bible. It certainly is true, by profession and predilection (courses on the New Testament remain at the heart of his activity), but we cannot forget the variety of his output (these different short works that we listed bear witness to this) nor his presence in contemporary issues. In the Middle Ages, theology, "queen of sciences," could not be disinterested by them, and Thomas says nothing that would lead us believe that his correspondents force him to go beyond the limits of his knowledge. To this multiform activity, we must add this final feature: Thomas is also the commentator on Aristotle.

THE COMMENTATOR ON ARISTOTLE

This final major occupation of Thomas's second time teaching in Paris, which had begun with his commentary on Aristotle's *On the Soul* in the last year of his stay in Rome, continued in Paris at a more rapid pace. He must have had to pursue this task without a break, since the commentaries of Aristotle multiplied from this point on. Without pretending to follow a chronological order—which is difficult to determine, since certain books had been written entirely in Paris and others begun in Paris and continued in Naples and still others left aside—we can list in first place the *Book of Interpretation* (often referred to according to its Greek title *Peri Hermeneias*) followed by the *Second Analytics*, both of which, in Aristotle, are part of a much larger whole, called *Organon*, "working instruments," which was about how to arrive at a correct reflection. Thomas's commentary follows along these lines, and, in spite of their very technical character, these two works had a broad audience.

With the *Commentaries on Physics* and *Metaphysics*, we approach the major works of this kind of commentary. Their titles are sufficient, and we can hardly say more. However, the *Commentary on the Nicomachean Ethics* (*Sententia libri Ethicorum*) lends itself better to a correct appreciation of Thomas's efforts with respect to Aristotle. Without going into details on its content—for that would require retracing the major elements of Thomas's ethics—we can understand better that he did not want to do a simple critical commentary, since it is clear that Thomas does not rely on himself. We cannot reproach him, for between Thomas's and Aristotle's respective moral systems is found the profound difference brought by the Gospels. While Aristotle proceeds according to a fundamentally pagan ethic, Thomas is situated within a Christian perspective and manages to make Aristotle say that the contemplative finality in which Thomas sees himself is the happiness of the final beatitude. We will no doubt understand better what he wanted to do if we recall that this *Commentary on Ethics* was not a course that he would have given to his students. Rather, it was the equivalent of a personal reading with a pen in his hand in order to force himself to dig deeply into Aristotle's text so as to prepare himself for composing the moral part of the *Summa theologiae*.

Beyond these major works, Thomas left behind various other writings that he had not finished, including the beginnings of a *Commentary on Politics*, strongly denounced by posterity because his critics wanted to complete it from a standpoint that was quite different from Thomas's. The *Commentary on Heaven and Earth* is clearly about cosmology; if Thomas had completed it according to his own metaphysical views, which always deserve to be known, the "scientific" data are today largely outdated. When reading it, we can see that here, more than anywhere else, Thomas reinterprets Aristotle according to the Christian faith, as was seen with his return to the question of the *Eternity of the World*. The *Commentary on Generation and Corruption* is not only not finished, but scarcely begun. In his deposition at the trial in Naples, Guillaume de Tocco swears that he saw Thomas in the process of writing this work and he even believes that it was his last work on philosophy. Thus, it would be at Naples in 1272 or 1273, in the final months of Thomas's activity (before December 1273). It was also at this time that we find another incomplete work, *On Meteors*.

Thomas and His Secretaries

We will come back to Thomas's behavior with respect to Aristotle and on what he owes him. With the end of his stay in Paris, the moment has come to pause in order to return to a question that is very difficult to avoid. On its own, the list of commentaries of Aristotle's writing is enough to witness to the intensity of the work accomplished by Thomas and, of course, the speed at which he did it. The final part of our chapter on the Roman period already underscored the great quantity of work accomplished by Thomas during these three years. If we now take a retrospective look at Thomas's production during his second stay in Paris, we can only be struck with astonishment. A recap of his work during this period ends, in fact, with the following list: *Commentaries on Matthew* and *On John*; the enormous *Second Part of the Summa theologiae* in its entirety, in addition to twenty-five questions of the *Third Part*, ten or so commentaries on Aristotle, of which some were left unfinished, but some very lengthy, to which we must add the commentary *On the Book of Causes*, the *Questions on Evil* (101 articles) and *On the Virtues* (36 articles) plus a series of seven *Quodlibets* (176 articles), a series of fourteen "opuscules," among which are the *Eternity of the World*, the *Unity of the Intellect*, the *Perfection of the Spiritual Life*, *Against Those Who Lead Astray*, *Separate Substances*, and still others.

If the historical probabilities—and sometimes certitudes—were not as strong, it is not only astonishment that this list provokes, but disbelief as well. Thus, we have to wonder and attempt to determine if such a thing is even materially possible, and under what conditions. For this, we will appeal to some numbers for which we would like to ask pardon, knowing that their display is reduced to a minimum. So we will consider them with circumspection, given the incertitude of the exact dates of certain writings. The sums found in the *Index Thomisticus*—an outdated reference work, due to the fact that we can find on the Internet all of the texts and words of Thomas's works—which, on the one hand is very precise, and on the other hand, the margin of error makes it, in the end, rather weak.

The numerical assessment of the work done during the period that runs from October 1268 to the end of April 1272, that is, roughly 1,253 possible days of work, allows us to arrive at a total of 4,061 pages, according to the very compact written edition. This is equal, on average, to a little more than three pages a day, or a daily total of 2,403 words. If we consider only the sixteen months of the final period (1271–1272)—taking into account the fact that certain works overlapped more or less from January 1, 1271—the number rises to approximately 2,747 pages written over 466 days, at a daily rate of six pages, clearly superior to the earlier computation. A final number will perhaps help us to visualize the work that Thomas accomplished: a sheet of our actual paper (format A4) with small letters typed on it means that Thomas would have written more than 12 pages per day. Now, with the exception perhaps of popular novelists, no writer in this domain wherein Thomas moved can boast of having written one third of that. Imagine that, at only two pages per day, we could end up with the equivalent of two books of 350 pages per year.

This result cannot be explained by Thomas's work alone. As we have written earlier, we have to remind ourselves of the team of secretaries that he had at his disposal. It became a palpable necessity. Attested to from his first stay in Paris, the presence of these secretaries is constantly referred to thereafter. The hand of Raynald, a longtime companion, is recognizable in several manuscripts; the same can be said of Jacobin d'Asti. While it is not possible always to identify their handwriting, we know the names of several among them: Raymond Severi, Nicolas de Marsillac, and Pierre d'Andria were all Domincans; Evenus, a member of the secular clergy, could have been a professional, while Léger de Besançon, the one who provided a clean copy of the lessons *On Matthew*, seems to have been merely one of Thomas's students.

Tocco often repeats that Thomas hired the most competent secretaries of his time to write or to take dictation. We can hazard that the second occupation came to predominate with time, for the rare autographs that have come down to us are those that belonged to the first part of his career (*On Isaiah, On Boethius, Sentences III*); the *Summa contra Gentiles* seems to be the last example known. Thomas must have noticed very early on that his own handwriting was impossible to make out for even a trained scribe. But we have proof of the existence of these secretaries from the beginning of his teaching, and we also know that he was in the habit of dictating to several people.

Thus, Bartholomew of Capua, recounting the way that Thomas organized his day, reports that after having said Mass and taught his class, "he would settle down to write and to dictate to several secretaries." Tocco also gives voice to the same fact that he pretends to have learned from the "trustworthy relationship of his companion, Raynald, of his students and of his secretaries," according to whom Thomas would, at the same time, "dictate on several diverse matters to three and sometimes four secretaries." We should not, however, take this too literally: the presence of several secretaries around Thomas does not mean that he dictated simultaneously to several persons. The concentration that these matters required, means that it is highly unlikely that he went from one to another, as one would say of certain celebrities who would have thus dictated their mail. Rather, one should think of persons who followed each other in his service during the course of a day in order to satisfy Thomas's work schedule. They were obliged to take turns, for according to the witness of specialists, a scribe could not copy more than one folio per day. If Thomas's legendary concentration was the indispensable condition to complete all of these works, one should equally think of a veritable organization and even a rationalization of work. The secretaries can be employed in other tasks than stenography. We can guess this from the writing of the *Golden Chain* and the considerable research for documents that this would have entailed. We get a little closer with the *Questions on Truth*—where one speaks of the note cards that Thomas used—and one can touch it, so to speak, with the *Table of Ethics*, where we have, in a near original state, the work of the secretaries before Thomas revised it.

We shall not get very far by supposing that the secretaries had simply prepared the material so that the master had nothing more to do than tidy it up. Any professor who has benefited from the collaboration of a competent assistant will understand without difficulty how these things work. We can therefore describe Thomas's collaborators organized into a veritable workshop of literary production—according to the well-known example of the schools of painting. There is hardly any other way to explain Thomas's output in a reasonable fashion. According to the description of his days and other details, we hardly need to look at the texts in order to understand, as well, that Thomas did not lose a minute of work. When they refer to his literary output, his biographers willingly see something of the miraculous; if indeed there was a miracle, we should perhaps place it in the context that he maintained this rhythm and with a growing intensity for some twenty-five years.

BENESCRIPSISTI THOMA

LAST TIME TEACHING
IN NAPLES, 1272–1273

Thomas left Paris in the spring of 1272 after an almost four year stay. As is very often the case when it comes to dates, we must confess a relative lack of certitude. It is certain that Thomas could still have held his *quodlibet* discussions of Lent 1272; still, shortly after Pentecost of the same year (June 12, 1272), the Chapter of the Province of Rome, meeting in Florence, assigned him the task of organizing a school of theology, leaving him the free choice of place, personnel, and number of students. This decision is an indication of the fact that he had already returned, or was on the point of returning to Italy. Several documents attest to his presence in Naples from September 10, 1272.

Contrary to what we may believe, the choice of Naples as the place of establishing a new school of studies entrusted to him was not for Thomas a subjective matter. In fact, this site had been chosen three years earlier by a previous Chapter, and preparatory work had undoubtedly been undertaken: a minimum of organization had already been put into place in order to welcome students sent by their monasteries in the provinces. Moreover, Naples was the residence of the most powerful of the Italian princes and the only city to have a certain university tradition since its foundation by Frederick II and the attempt at restoration by Charles I of Anjou. In a letter of July 31, 1272, Charles sought to profit from the ongoing rampant strikes in Paris and invited masters and students to come to his city—whose charms and services he praises—to continue their studies. We know of at least three masters who allowed themselves to be convinced. From other sources, we know that Thomas will receive one ounce of gold per month for teaching theology. Still, this new Dominican center at Naples will have neither the importance nor the juridical status of Paris or Bologna, Padua or Montpellier, cities in which the studium of mendicants effectively continued the faculty of theology of the University.

Course on the Epistles of Saint Paul

As for the matter taught during these last months of Thomas's life, all indications that we have at our disposal lead us to believe that he taught a course on the Psalter and another on the Epistles of Saint Paul or, more precisely, on his *Letter to the Romans*. The information that we have on the dates and the site of teaching from commentaries on different epistles—which had been discussed at length—have recently been completely rethought, and it is certain that the *Letter to the Romans* was being taught at this period. Thomas's direct contribution maintains the traces that he had made in the first thirteen chapters of his commentary. These were not arbitrary interventions due to copyists or editors who guided their work, as often happens, but rather quick corrections by the author that the confused scribes had trouble putting in their precise place because they had been badly noted. Based on the observations that we can discern from the manuscripts in the question, we can add the statements of an oracular witness. When this witness speaks about classes on all of the epistles of Paul, the historian, Ptolemy de Lucques, reserves a special place for the *Letter to the Romans*, adding: "I saw and read this text which [Thomas] himself annotated." Everything indicates that Thomas had, indeed, taught at Naples on the *Letter to the Romans* and that he corrected the first thirteen chapters rapidly. It is from Naples that the text was disseminated, as well as, without a doubt, the text of Paul's corpus.

For writings other than the *Letter to the Romans*, things are less clear. We can at least stress that, in spite of the diversity of time and place, Thomas considered his Pauline commentary as a whole. The proof for this is found in the Prologue that he placed at the beginning of the entire work. There, he lays out a general plan of all of the epistles according to which each responds to a precise outline, and he refers to this plan at the top of each epistle, which highlights the unity of his proposal. Here is a lengthy passage of the text that provides at the same time a very clear example and meaning of his method:

> The Apostle wrote fourteen epistles: nine of which instruct the Church of the Gentiles; four the prelates and the princes of the Church, as well as the kings; the last is addressed to the Hebrews, the sons of Israel. This teaching is entirely about

the grace of Christ that we can examine by means of three modes.

First of all, according to what we find in the Prologue itself, Christ, and this is how he is called in the *Epistle to the Hebrews*. Then, according to how he is in the principal members of the Mystical Body, and it is thus that we find him in the epistles addressed to the prelates (the Pastoral Letters). Finally, according to how he is in the Mystical Body itself, which is the Church, and thus we find him in the epistle addressed to the Gentiles.

[In the last case], there is another distinction, for Christ's grace admits of a triple consideration. First, in itself, as we find in the *Epistle to the Romans*. Second, in the sacraments of grace, as we find in the two *Epistles to the Corinthians*—the first of which deals with the sacraments themselves and the second with the dignity of their ministers—and in the *Epistle to the Galatians*, from which are excluded superfluous sacraments (Jewish customs) against those who wanted to add the ancient sacraments (circumcision) again. Third, Christ's grace is considered according to the work of unity that it brings about in the Church.

[From this last point of view], the Apostle first deals with the foundation of ecclesial unity in the *Epistle to the Ephesians*; after that, of its confirmation and progress in the *Epistle to the Philippians*; then, of its defense against errors in the *Epistle to the Colossians*, against the present persecutions in the *First Epistle to the Thessalonians*, against future persecutions and especially the time of the Antichrist in the second.

As for the prelates of the Church, he instructs both the spiritual and the temporal. For the spiritual, he speaks about the foundation, the construction and the governance of the ecclesiastical unity in the *First Epistle to Timothy*, of firmness in the face of persecutors in the second, in defense against the heretics in the *Epistle to Titus*. As for temporal lords, he instructs them in his *Epistle to Philemon*.

Here then is the reason for the distinction and the order of all of the epistles.

The modern reader, used to a completely different approach to the Bible, whether it be scientific or pastoral, cannot help but be surprised when confronted with Thomas's systematic presentation. Thomas does not seem to realize that the letters of Paul are only occasional writings and that nothing could be further from the Apostle's thought than to transmit a teaching so strongly structured around the grace of Christ. On the other hand, we should not believe that he was more naïve than he was and to think that he believed himself to have captured all of the richness of Paul's text.

This long text not only shows the unity of Thomas's proposal; it also shows to what extent the ecclesial perspective is present in his thought. This remains important if we are to understand something of his spiritual theology. It is sufficient to go through his *Commentaries* in order to find in them numerous indications pointing in that direction. Here are a few lines on the Holy Spirit that correspond to the text on Christ that we have just cited. Concerning Romans 8:2: "The law of the Spirit who gives life in Christ Jesus," Thomas writes the following:

The first meaning is that the law is the Holy Spirit Himself. In such a way that by the law of the Spirit we must understand the law that is the Spirit. In effect, the law's purpose is to incite us to do good. According to Aristotle, the intention of the law-giver is to make good citizens; now human law cannot do this except by making known what the good is that one must do. The Holy Spirit, Himself, who lives in the soul, not only teaches what we must do by enlightening the intelligence, He also inclines the will to act justly.... A second meaning, this law can be understood as the proper effect of the Holy Spirit, meaning faith as it acts through love. He also teaches interiorly what we must do, according to 1 John 2:20: *But you have an anointing from the Holy Spirit*; He moves the will to action, according to 2 Corinthians 5:14: *For the love of Christ impels us.* This law is therefore called the new law because it is identified with the Holy Spirit, either because the Spirit Himself works in us.... And if the Apostle adds in Christ Jesus, it is because this Spirit is given only to those who are in Christ Jesus. As the natural breath of life does not reach the member that is not connected to the Head, so in the same way the Holy Spirit does not reach the member who is not connected to his leader, the Christ.

Course on the Psalter

If we exclude Thomas's pursuit of the writing of *Summa theologiae* (IIIa q. 20/25–90), we do not know what would have been Thomas's other academic activities during 1272–1274. As for materials taught, since we have just said what happened with the end of the Pauline writings, this leaves us to speak about the course on the Psalter. Historians, for a long time, have hesitated on this late date in Thomas's career; the latest research has shown that the number of allusions that Thomas makes in his class on the Psalter to his previous work no longer leaves any doubt.

As for the content, the prologue to this course is one of the most instructive for grasping the method and intention of the author, who prepares himself to comment on this treasury of ecclesial prayer. Just as enlightening as that on Saint Paul quoted above, it is complementary to it and illustrates the way in which Thomas approaches his diverse commentaries on Scripture. He wants to highlight the "cause," which is fourfold: matter, form, purpose, agent, according to the teaching of Aristotle:

> "Its matter is universal; while each of the other canonical books has its special matter, this one covers the matter of all of theology." [This can be verified in several areas, especially in that which concerns the work of salvation accomplished by Christ]. Everything that touches on the end of the Incarnation is expressed in this book in such a clear manner that it is like having the Gospel in front of us, not Prophecy.... This fullness is the reason why the Church ceaselessly returns to the Psalter, for it contains all of Scripture.

After the matter, it is time to characterize the mode or the form of this book:

> In fact, the mode of Holy Scriptures is multiple. It can be "narrative" ... as in the Historical Books; "memorative," "exhortative," and "prescriptive" ... as in the Law, the Prophets or Wisdom Literature; "disputative" ... as in the Book of Job or in Saint Paul; and, finally, "critical" or "laudatory" as in the Psalms. Indeed, all which, in the other Books, is treated according the mode specified can be discovered here in the form of praises and prayer.... It is from this that the Book takes its title: The Beginning of the Book of Hymns, or the "soliloquies" of the prophet David regarding Christ. The hymn is a praise of God under the form of chant. Chant is the exultation of the soul regarding eternal realities expressed with the voice. It teaches us to praise God joyfully. The soliloquy is the personal colloquy of man with God or else with oneself; this is proper to the one who praises or prays.
>
> As for the end of this Scripture, it is prayer, the elevation of the soul to God.... It is possible for the soul to raise itself to God in four ways: (1) In order to admire the grandeur of His power ...: elevation of faith; (2) In order to reach out to

the excellence of His eternal happiness . . . : elevation of hope; (3) In order to attach oneself closely to His divine goodness and holiness . . . : elevation of charity; (4) In order to imitate the divine justice in one's way of acting . . . : elevation of justice. [These different points are hinted at in diverse psalms], and that is why Saint Gregory assures us that if psalmody is accompanied by the intention of the heart, it prepares in the soul a way to God, who infuses in it the mysteries of prophecy or the grace of compunction.

As for the author of this work, it is clearly God Himself, since the Holy Scriptures are not the fruit of human willing, but of divine inspiration that creates the appropriate instruments. Thomas thus ends his introduction with several indications on the way that prophetic revelation is brought about while still reserving the play of secondary causes. Whoever spends time in this "reading" of the psalms by Thomas will not regret it. Its dryness leaves one to guess that the scribe barely noted the essential ideas of the master, leaving aside the more circumstantial explanations as well as the warmth of the living word that makes oral teaching something completely different from scribbling class notes, no matter how well taken they are. One has to know how to read this text so that it can deliver a little of its richness, return to its sources and go and see what Gregory or Augustine says about a passage in order to reconstitute, if possible, what Thomas had to say in his course.

Here is an example of how—with respect to Psalm 3:6: *I lie down and I sleep*—Thomas evokes with a word the birth of the Church from the pierced side of Christ sleeping the sleep of death, signified by the birth of Eve from Adam's side at the dawn of creation. Here, Thomas echoes a veritable patristic common-place, which extends the Pauline parallel between the two Adams by a notion dear to Irenaeus of the two Eves—the

Church being the new "mother of the living"—and which was conveyed to him by two familiar authors, Augustine and Chrysostom, whose texts are of a rare depth. Thomas's listeners knew these texts, or at least would have heard them from his own lips. In the absence of an adequate commentary, today's reader risks missing the richness of this background. Analogous examples could be multiplied with regards to prayer, affectivity, the desire for God, etc.

The translations of Thomas's scriptural commentaries have multiplied since the end of the previous century, but still there remains a lot to be done before they are more utilized and find their way into current day practical theology. As well done as these translations are, they will not be fully useful or fruitful if they are not followed up with and extended by their integration in theological reflection, for the difficulty lies less with Latin than with what is not said in the texts.

The "Mysteries" of the Life of Christ

In leaving Paris, Thomas brought with him a certain number of books to work on. Among the tasks that still awaited him, he had certainly and firstly to finish the *Summa*. At his arrival in Naples, the only portions of the *Third Part* that had been written were the first twenty or twenty-five questions. What corresponds more or less to the properly speculative part of the theology of Christ: the study of the union of the two natures, human and divine, in the unique person of Christ, and what this means for how we speak of him. Thus, it was at Naples that Thomas wrote the end of the questions on Christ and the beginning of the theology of the sacraments. We can leave aside the questions on sacramental theology, but we must speak, however briefly, of this part of his Christology.

Popularized in the past under the inexact title of the *Life of Christ*, questions 27–59 of the *Third Part* reveal a surprising return to the scriptural and patristic sources after the high level of speculative theology in questions 1–26. For those who are familiar with Thomas's scriptural commentaries and the great effort needed in researching the Fathers of the Church represented by the *Golden Chain*, there is, on the contrary, nothing surprising in this. We have to speak of this in some depth, since this part has the newest teaching about Christology and is also one of the two greatest original sections of the *Summa*, after his doctrine on man. Moreover, we can also see more than one confluence between these pages and Thomas's evolution in the last months of his life.

Thomas says that he wants to speak about "what the Son of God incarnate did and suffered in his human nature to which it is united," or—according to a formula that occurs several times—"of all that Christ did and lived during his life on earth." The plan that he introduces is developed in four sections, whose format, as we will see, is that of the entire *Summa theologiae* itself:

- Entrance (*ingressus*) of the Son of God into this world (questions 27–39). It is here that he speaks of Jesus' mother, the Virgin Mary, of her sanctification in the womb of her mother, of her marriage with Joseph (a true marriage), of the annunciation of the angel, etc. This is not meant to be a complete theology of the Virgin Mary, for the principal focus is on Christology, and everything else is seen in relationship to the birth of Jesus and to the various circumstances connected to it. Along with some out-of-date physiological data, there are some surprising intuitions (Mary giving her consent to the coming of the Savior in the name of the entire human race: "in the name of all of human nature").

- The unfolding *(progressus)* of his life in this world (questions 40–45) takes up what we commonly call Christ's public life, the kind of life he led and the teaching that we can garner for those who wish to announce his message today; his temptation in the desert and its meaning in the history of salvation, his teaching, his miracles, and his transfiguration.

- His exit *(exitus)* from this world, his passion and death (questions 46–52). Under agreed upon Scholastic titles, Thomas treats the most burning questions, which are still discussed today in the theology of redemption. As for the actors in the passion (the "efficient cause," says Aquinas), he asks about their respective responsibilities, not only that of the Jews or the Romans, but that of the human race in general and even that of the Father, who first "delivered" Jesus. The efficient modality of the passion—the way in which it effects salvation—puts in place with precision the notions of merit, satisfaction, sacrifice, redemption, saving for Christ alone to be the "Redeemer," for the person of the Word alone could give to human action such a value.

- Exaltation *(exaltation)*, or his triumph after this life (questions 53–59). These last questions look closely at the final disposition of Christ's mystery: the resurrection, ascension, sitting at the right hand of the Father and the capacity then given to Christ to be equal to the Father—and with his humanity—the judge of the living and the dead.

This simple enumeration of some of the themes treated gives us a better glimpse of what the author's real proposal was. The succession of the gospel stories gave him a valuable historical framework. It allowed him to review all of the events of Jesus' life (he always says, "the Christ"), both the small and the great, giving him the opportunity to deal with misunderstood subjects by a number of theologians, such as the baptism, Christ's temptations, or his manner of living among the crowds. Thomas wants to show that the Word became man in the most human manner, and that there is material here not only for theological reflection, but for unending repetition in order to deepen the mystery of the Incarnation and to illuminate the Christian life by means of spiritual meditation. It is a deliberate return to the Gospels, for "it is there that the substance of the Catholic faith and the norm for all of our Christian life is given to us."

Unlike some theologians of the Counter-Reformation, whether Protestant or Catholic, who seemed to reduce the work of salvation to the pinnacle of suffering and death, Thomas does not think that Christ's birth and the humble years of his hidden life are a superfluous preface to his death on the cross as if this were the only thing that counted. Nothing was more foreign to him than this attention to Christ's suffering, and he repeats peacefully: "The least sufferings (*minima passio*) of Christ would have sufficed to redeem the human race." In fact, in many places, this word *passio* retains its initial etymological meaning and does not necessarily mean "suffering," but rather everything that the Word did and suffered, felt, and lived in our human condition. Thomas the theologian, so often believed to be too abstract, knows the weight of the historical insertion of the Word into our humanity, and it is this that he endeavors to highlight.

To give it its real name, which is what Thomas wished to do, it is a "theology of the mysteries" of Jesus' life. We will easily understand what this is about if we recall that Saint Paul's use of "mystery" (*mysterion*) (Ephesians 3:3), sums up at the same time Christ's life in itself and the way by which God's plan was fulfilled in Jesus. This is done in such a way that if the whole of Christ's life is itself the mystery of God's love, which makes itself known and active in history, each of his acts is also a "mystery" in the sense that it points to and brings to fruition this complete "mystery." Deeply traditional, Thomas's way of looking at things has its roots in the first Christian thinkers of the Christian faith. Nor was it not unknown among the Scholastics, whether their predecessors and contemporaries, to refer to this way on occasion. Still, Thomas shows himself here to be profoundly original, for he is the first and will be the only one for a long time to analyze these mysteries as an intelligible whole, at one and the same time autonomous and an integral part of his theological reflection on Christ.

As a way of illustrating these last remarks, it will be helpful to reproduce an example of how Thomas proceeds in this last part of the *Summa*. He examines the question, which for a long time had been traditional, whether God would have had at His disposal a more apt means than the Christ's passion to save the human race. Thomas could have been content to use abstract reason, but, on the contrary, he adopts a more concrete means:

> A means is "appropriate" to an end in the measure that it secures for [that end] the greatest number of advantages. Now, because man had been saved by Christ's passion, this passion, beyond freedom from sin, secured for him many advantages for his salvation.
>
> By means of it, humans know how much God loves them and by this they are moved to love Him, and it is in this love that the perfection of the salvation of humans consists. Thus, Saint Paul says (Romans 5:8): "The proof that God loves us is that Christ, while we were still sinners, died for us."
>
> By means of the passion, Christ gave us an example of obedience, humility, constancy, justice, and the other virtues

necessary for human salvation. As Saint Peter says (1 Peter 2:21): "Christ suffered for us leaving us an example that we should follow in his steps."

Christ, by his passion, not only delivered us from sin; in addition, he also merited for us the grace of justification and the glory of beatitude.

Because of his passion, humans understand that they have a duty to keep themselves pure from all sin when they think that they have been redeemed from sin by the blood of Christ, according to Saint Paul (1 Corinthians 6:20): "You have been bought at a great price! Glorify God in your bodies."

The passion conferred on humans a higher dignity: conquered and deceived by the devil, humans would conquer him in turn; having deserved death, they would also, in dying, triumph over death itself, and Saint Paul tells us (1 Corinthians 15:57): "Give thanks to God for having given us the victory through Jesus Christ."

For all of these reasons, it was "appropriate" and therefore better that we were freed by the passion of Christ than by God simply willing it.

This text, chosen from among many others of equal significance, is interesting in that it shows, in act, the theologian's method in this part of his writing. He does not try to prove the necessity of the passion (he himself said that the passion was not "necessary" in the strict sense); rather, the passion is a fact; he wants to highlight what he calls its "appropriateness." Knowing everything that he knows elsewhere of God's plan for humanity, he seeks to emphasize all of the reasons that allow us to understand [the passion] as a supreme act of Christ's and God's love of humanity. He reconstructs a network of convergences that suggest that such an act, clearly beyond reason, is not, however, without reason. Here, the theology is no longer *demonstrative* (in truth, theology is rarely this), but, rather, it is *ostensive* (from the Latin verb *ostendere* which means "to show"). Thomas shows to those who wish to see that it is exactly [the passion] that the texts of Revelation affirm and that this is the reason one has to be closely committed to the text of Holy Scriptures (here, four out of five arguments are taken directly from the New Testament; elsewhere, the texts of the Fathers are used at the same rate).

Within the same movement, theology also becomes exhortative (in keeping with what we read in the Prologue regarding the course on the Psalms): this inducement to love on the part of God cannot remain without effect in the theologian—nor on the part of his reader! How true it is that, for Thomas, a well-done theology reaches its climax in spirituality and in the Church's pastoral life:

> Whoever wants to lead a perfect life has nothing to do other than to despise what Christ despised when on the cross and to desire what he desired. In fact, there is no single example of virtue that the cross did not give us. Are you looking for an example of charity? There is no greater love than to give one's life for their friends, and Christ did this on the cross.... Are you looking for an example of patience? The most perfect is that on the cross. Are you looking for an example of humility? Look at the Crucified. An example of obedience? Put yourself in the footsteps the one who made himself obedient until death.... An example of disdain for worldly things? Walk behind him who is the Lord of lords and King of kings, in whom is found all the treasures of wisdom and who yet, on the cross, appears naked, the object of mockery, spat upon, slapped, crowned with thorns, his thirst quenched with gall and vinegar, put to death.

We will come back to this omnipresence of Christ as the absolute model of the Christian life; for now, it is enough to know that Thomas never ceases recalling that "every action of Christ is for us an instruction," which was a rule of life for Thomas himself.

Last Months and Death of Thomas

If our proposal had been to write a biography, the moment would be here to read the most concrete chapter of this book. Indeed, the return to Naples provides us with the opportunity to meet Thomas in a setting that was familiar to him, to meet the members of this family, others who knew him or heard him preaching, who described what he looked like or how he acted in his relationships with others, and who brought their witness to his process of canonization. No other moment of his life has been so clearly spelled out as that of his last months. Still, we have to forego this and settle—however briefly—for looking at some complementary elements to what we have already said.

In fact, Thomas continued to be very taken up by other tasks than those of direct instruction and of finishing the *Summa*. As was the case in all of the other places where we have seen him at work, others continued to solicit from him other activities (sometimes very far from teaching, as the fact of having been designated as the executor of his brother-in-law, Roger of Aquila!). He still had different works to finish, and they will remain incomplete as, for instance, his commentaries on Aristotle, about which we have already spoken. We know also that during this period he preached, at least two imposing series of sermons on the *Ten Commandments* and the *Our Father*, to the faithful of the conventual church of Naples and in his own language, as the witnesses to his canonization have assured us.

On September 29, 1273, Thomas participates again at the Chapter of his province in Rome in the capacity of "definer," charged with others to "define" the policies of the Province for the period that was to come. Several weeks later, while he was celebrating Mass in the Chapel of Saint Nicholas, he experienced a new ecstasy (he already had had others during the preceding day), and he left the chapel profoundly transformed: "After this Mass, he would never write anything else again, nor would he dictate anything else, and he even left his writing materials; he was in the midst of the third part of the *Summa*, his treatise on penitence." To a stupefied Raynald, who did not understand why Thomas had abandoned his work, the Master answered simply, "I can no longer." Returning to his duties, Raynald receives the same response: "I can no longer do it. Everything that I have written seems to be straw in comparison to what I have seen." This was around the time of the Feast of Saint Nicholas (December 6, 1273).

These words are universally known by those who are interested even a tiny bit in Thomas Aquinas, but they are often misunderstood. The expression, "Everything that I have written seems to be straw in comparison" does not mean that it is all is worth nothing. We could, in fact, ask ourselves if it would be worth the effort to study his work if that were the case. We would be deceiving ourselves if we thought so. In reality, straw is the consecrated expression for distinguishing, according to its full meaning, the grain of reality that envelops these words. Words are not reality; they designate it and lead to it. Arriving at reality itself, Thomas had some right to feel detached from his own words. It certainly does not mean that he considered his work as worthless. He had simply arrived beyond it.

After some time at his sister's, where he had been sent to rest, Thomas and his companion returned to Naples. Several weeks later, he had to travel again for the council that Gregory X had convoked in Lyons for May 1, 1274, in view of a meeting with the Greeks. So Thomas brought with him the *Summa contra Gentiles* that he had written at the request of Urban IV. The reputation of the traveler traveled faster than he did, and he was met by an envoy of Bernard l'Ayglier, the abbot of Monte Cassino, who invited him to take a short detour to the abbey in order to enlighten his religious on the meaning of a passage of Saint Gregory. Already very tired, Thomas declined the offer of stopping at the monastery, arguing that a written response will have the advantage of being useful to future readers and not simply to those in the present.

The monks are troubled by the interpretation of a text that concerns the relationship between the infallibility of divine foreknowledge and human freedom. Thomas reaffirms these two points and underscores that the difference in plan between the two terms in the present brings with it no necessity of one over the other: to see someone sitting does obligate him to sit. Thus God cannot deceive himself in His knowledge, which sees everything in the present of His eternity, and man remains free in his activity situated in time. Paradoxically, this letter to Bernard Ayglier, abbot of Monte Cassino, dictated to Raynald, is perhaps the clearest and shortest that Thomas has ever given on this problem. He is already exhausted by sickness, but his intellectual faculties are still intact.

He will die a few days later at the Cistercian abbey of Fossanova, where he had stopped to get his strength back. After having confessed to Raynald, he received for the last time Christ on earth.

BENESCRIPSISTI THOMA·

THOMAS'S
SOURCES

The purpose of this small book is to facilitate a first approach to Thomas Aquinas's work. If one wants to go a bit beyond this rapid sketch, we have to take a further step. Perhaps this will not be the easiest, since we will not have the backing of biographical material about his life to go through or a work to discover. But if we want to go beyond an unjustifiable timeless presentation, this chapter will allow us to see a little better how Thomas is placed in the history of human thought.

In fact, one suspects Thomas is not an absolute starting point. As all of the thinkers who have succeeded one another since Antiquity, he is an heir of those who preceded him. In his case, these last are particularly numerous. "To read Thomas

Aquinas consists in dealing with a forest of authors where philosophers and theologians push together" (T.-D. Humbrecht). In fact, if we believe the patient counting done by various scholars, the list of the Greek or Latin ancient authors, pagan or Christian, Arab or Jew, whom Thomas used in his complete works totals 164 names. We have to add to this number the biblical citations, unidentified anonymous writers, heretics, names only occasionally cited, liturgical citations, and the lives of the saints. A complete list of works that Thomas could have read in their entirety has yet to be made. It is certain that, in spite of the breadth of his knowledge, he did not read all of them, for the simple reason that he did not have all of these books at hand. For the most part, he must have settled for what he found in the glosses that came with the Bible or in the florilegia that had already been assembled or had been established for the needs of the *Golden Chain*.

It would be out of the question to review this enormous amount of material or even only a part of it. It will be more judicious of us to concern ourselves with the way in which Thomas handled this patrimony. When we talk about the sources of his thought, we must first of all specify that the word does not have exactly the same meaning as for us. For sure, there are authors who influenced him in a more general way, like Aristotle or Saint Augustine, but like all of his contemporaries, the use of authors who preceded him takes the form of a recourse to "authorities," meaning not simply an evocation of these authors, but more precisely citations that summarize the thought of these authors. For example, when he speaks about the authority of Scripture, or that of Augustine or Aristotle in a given context, he thinks first of a citation that represents more than a simple reference, an authorized position that one must take into account.

Thomas explained this matter in a few texts that allow him to rank his sources according to their greater or lesser proximity with respect to the faith. At the top of the list come the authorities taken for Holy Scripture: the Word of God confers on its authors an absolute principle. This is why even if the use of the argument from authority is the weakest in human reason, as Boethius says, it is fitting, on the contrary, in theology because theology is founded on divine Revelation. In second place come the authorities of the Fathers of the Church, when they comment on a given revelation; their authority is certainly great in the domain of the faith, and on other matters, they could err. Thomas holds them in high esteem: when they speak the truth, they bear witness to the grandeur of the human spirit. Just as grace does not destroy nature, reason itself is not contrary to the faith, and so it is legitimate to have recourse to the philosophers; they can contribute to an understanding of revelation.

HOLY SCRIPTURE

Scripture is the only source that has absolute value, for it is the organ of Revelation, the place where we find the divine truth expressed in human terms. That which depends on God's free will (the Incarnation of the Word, for example) goes beyond what is due to our nature: this can be known only insofar as it is transmitted to us by Holy Scripture. For Thomas, "The Holy Scripture is the rule of faith to which nothing can be added or subtracted." We ought not to expand with our additions, nor decrease it by our omissions, nor pervert it with our evil commentaries. The Creed also carries the title of "rule of faith," which comes from the fact that it is almost entirely composed of phrases taken from Holy Scripture. When we carefully keep the holy words, it is they who keep us and affirm us in obedience.

This reference to Scripture is so strong that Thomas goes so far as to say: "We do not believe in the successors to the apostles and prophets except to the extent that they proclaim to us what the apostles and prophets left us in their writings."

The authority of Scripture must not, however, be understood univocally. The task of the master who teaches is not limited to repeating words in a servile way. This would even be the negation of the goal pursued by the teacher. Now we know that Thomas's principal activity, in conformity with his title of Master of Sacred Scripture, was to explain the Bible. Numerous passages shed light on the way that Thomas deals with his principal source. He first makes clear the plurality of the meaning of Scripture.

If the Bible has several meanings, it is because it is not a book like others. The intention of the principal author can go beyond the conscious intention of the human author, who serves as an instrument. Then comes a fundamental distinction:

> The author of Holy Scripture is God. He has the power to use not only words to express something, which humans can also do, but things as well. This is why it is common to all knowledge to express itself with words, knowledge has this property: that the things signified by the words have themselves also a signification.
>
> The first meaning, according to which words signify realities, come from the first meaning: it is the historical or literal meaning. The second meaning, according to which realities signified by words signify in their turn other realities, comes from the second meaning, called the spiritual (or allegorical) meaning, which is grounded in the literal meaning and presupposes it.

It would take us it too far astray to delve into the three subdivisions of the spiritual sense that follows (allegorical, moral, analogical), but we should at least know one thing: that it is God who is the principal author of this Book, and nothing can impede the same passage from having several literal meanings. Thomas grants to the literal sense a much wider breadth than those that we would spontaneously give. Here is a good example of this:

> The parabolic meaning is included in the literal meaning, for by the words we can signify something in its proper sense and something in its figural sense. In this case, the literal sense does not designate the figure itself, but what it represents. When, in fact, Scripture speaks about God's arm, the literal sense is not that God has a bodily arm, but what is signified by this member, namely, an active power.

Many signs point to the extreme care that Thomas brings to his reading of the biblical text. He is attentive to the ideas and to theological teaching, of course, but also to words, the grammar, and the style, to the differences in translation from Hebrew to Greek or from Greek to Latin. Any one of his commentaries shows us that the references to a version other than that of the Latin text of St. Jerome belong by right to his method. We could write long lists of textual criticism, or other interpretations, or references to the language or customs of Jews and Greeks. Thomas knows how to provide to the letter all of the attention that it deserves. Scholars specify which Latin text Thomas used and his occasional recourse to "corrections," that is, those collections of learned notes on the then-current Latin translation, which had accumulated over the course of centuries. He also stresses strongly the "scrupulous care brought to the study of the proper meaning of words," the attention to grammar and to style, as well as to history, which is seen in his care to identify historical details (G. Dahan).

Another indication of the respect with which Thomas treats the biblical text goes beyond the purely scientific approach. It is in fact a "confessional" exegesis, that of a believer for whom the "Bible is explained by the Bible, the word of God" (G. Dahan). Thomas is not the first or the only one to proceed this way, but the scriptural citations in his case are particularly numerous: those that Paul makes to confirm his words, and those that Thomas makes to shed light on Paul. The latter have a three-fold objective: illustration, explanation, and deepening. The illustrative citation "prolongs and completes an annotation of the Pauline text"; they are the least numerous, but they are not simply decorative. The explicative citation sheds light on a verse by other similar verses taken from other biblical books. The citations directed toward a deepening of the text are the most numerous. They are of a doctrinal order and proceed most often by verbal concordances according to a process that we found in the "collations" *On Isaiah*. The doctrinal difficulties arise from two apparently contradictory verses and are resolved with the help of small dossiers in support of each of these two verses. Thomas highlights the difficulty of the question, shows its complex character and provides his own solution.

The "confessing" style of Thomas's exegesis is apparent in the fact that he reads the Bible with the mind of the Church. The primacy that he gives to the scriptural argument has nothing to do with a defense of "sola scriptura" as in the case of Luther later on. It is clear that Thomas is following a long line of commentators who came one after another since the beginning. He willingly admits his debt to them and often refers to them. We cannot list them all, but the names of Origen, Jerome, Hillary, Ambrose, Augustine, Gregory, Chrysostom, Pseudo-Chrysostom, Pseudo-Dionysius, and still others, reappear frequently. The *Gloss* in its various forms and Peter Lombard are the foundational sources that transmit a number of other citations. This constant reference to the Fathers of the Church does not rule out Thomas's recourse to secular authors, and, among them, Aristotle is used more frequently than any of the Fathers except Augustine, who takes first place.

FATHERS OF THE CHURCH

After Scripture, the second great source used by Thomas is made up of the doctors who explain the meaning of Scripture. The distinction that Thomas makes at once between the importance of Sacred Scripture and that of "other doctors" whose authority is relative (probable) is predicated on an uncontestable fact:

> This is because our faith rests on the revelation made to the apostles and prophets, who wrote the canonical books, and not on a revelation—if there is such a thing—that would have been made by other doctors. [Just as Saint Augustine said:] "The books of canonical Scripture are the only ones to which I grant such an honor, for I believe quite firmly that their authors are incapable of error in what they have written. The others, as eminent as they are in holiness and doctrine, if I read them, it is not because they have thought one thing or wrote another that I deem to be true.

It is usual to refer to the "Fathers of the Church" when talking about these doctors who explain Scripture; Thomas was more circumspect. He readily speaks of the "holy Fathers," by which he does not mean "Fathers of the faith," since Christ alone could bear this title: "The others we can call 'doctors' or 'expositors' of the faith, not 'fathers.'" Rather than "Fathers," Thomas prefers "saints" (*sancti*). The importance that he grants them comes from the fact that they preserve Holy Scripture intact and, afterwards, that they knew how to explain correctly what is contained in the articles of faith. Thomas is always careful to stress that the "Holy Scriptures are explained in the light of the same Spirit who inspired them," and he adds:

> As for those things that do not belong to the faith, the doc-
> tors said many things that came from their own sources and,
> in these matters, they can err. Their teaching does not have
> the same authority and we are not obliged to believe them.
> Canonical Scripture of the Old and the New Testaments
> alone can be believed.

As for how we can concretely determine the manner by which we can treat of the authorities of the Fathers of the Church, Thomas recommends a method in his *Against the Errors of the Greeks*. Recall that this book, written at the request of Urban IV, examines a considerable number of texts of Greek Orthodox provenance (112 texts taken from 27 authors). Thomas does not hesitate to say that he found in these texts "a number of useful statements that guarantee our faith." In order to understand them correctly, he reminds us of the rules of a good interpretation:

> In the writings of the ancient Fathers there are certain state-
> ments that seem dubious to theologians of our time. This can
> come from two things. First, the errors arising against the
> faith lead the holy doctors of the Church to express them-
> selves with more circumspection in the hopes of eliminating
> new errors. For example, it is clear that the holy doctors who
> lived before the error of Arius did not address the subject of
> the unity of the divine essence in a more exact way than the
> doctors who came later.

This first example, taken from the context of the Arian crisis, is particularly pertinent when it comes to Christ and the

Trinity. We can adequately appreciate the orthodoxy of previous authors before the Council of Nicaea (325) or Chalcedon (451) only in the light of councils that came after them. Nor can we read and fully comprehend the writings of Augustine on grace if we do not know that in the books that he published after the Pelagian heresy, he expressed himself with much more prudence on the subject of free will than he had done before. In order to take into account other similar cases, Thomas states a general rule that he himself consistently practiced:

> If, however, it happens that, in the words of the ancient doctors, certain things were expressed with less prudence than we do today, we should neither condemn nor reject them for this; nor should we continue to disseminate them: we should explain them respectfully.

This respectful explanation is the famous "reverential explanation" about which we may have heard people speak. This stereotypical formula is found expressed in similar ways in a number of places. Here, Thomas is referring to certain opinions that we should consider with caution. He writes elsewhere: "These ways of speaking must not be generalized as if they were exact; wherever we find them in the writings of the holy Doctors, we ought to interpret them piously." There are those who have mocked their way of speaking wrongly. The appeal to the historic context shows this well. This way of proceeding does not mean that we can make the authors say whatever we want. For Thomas, this is a true rule of interpretation.

Bad translations and the difference of meaning of certain apparently similar words are another possible reason that can prevent a good understanding of the texts. The same words can sometimes say different things in Greek or in Latin. Thomas states a second rule:

It belongs to the task of a good translator of things concerning the Catholic faith to translate in a way that respects the meaning while adapting one's style to the genius of the language one is translating. It is clear, in fact, that if one must explain in a vulgar language things that are translated literally from Latin, the interpretation will be quite inadequate if one sticks to a word for word translation. Even more reason why we should not be surprised that there persists a certain obscurity if one translates word for word from one language to another.

There is a third rule, which consists in appealing to the context of the author's thought. When a passage is difficult, it would be absurd to stick with an unthinking literalness; one must look for the *intention* of the author. This rich expression gave rise to long developments; for our immediate purpose, it is enough to know that the intention is simply what the author wants to say. Sometimes it is a refutation, as when the intention of Aristotle is set against an interpretation that Averroës gives to it. It is also a way of exonerating an author, by showing that what he means is less reprehensible than his words taken literally. This method is used more than one hundred times in Thomas's work, who speaks of the intention of Augustine, of Aristotle, of Denys, and others.

The reading of these texts allows for two observations. First, among the authors found in the *Index thomisticus*, "the intention of the author" is an expression proper to Thomas: no one else uses it. Then, trying to discover the intention of the author is closely tied to a search for truth: "To probe more attentively the intention of the author and to know what the truth of the subject is, we have to know that the Ancients thought differently." Thomas then reviews the great successive philosophical viewpoints of philosophical thought on the matter. At the end of this review, he gives his own answer, which answer is found in the development of this long quest. Having recourse to the intention of the author has nothing to do with an easy escape. In order to understand what an author means to say, we have to recall the truth from which he began his search and that he sought to express with more or less felicity given his intellectual heritage. It is precisely here that Thomas deems himself eventually authorized to interpret or to extend his thought.

Thomas's reverence with respect to the Fathers does not exclude the possibility of distancing himself from them on occasion. We can see this, for example, with respect to Cyril of Alexandria, who omits the ninth anathema against Nestorius on the relationship of Christ and the Holy Spirit. Thomas understood what Cyril meant to say, but rather than going into a lengthy clarification, he preferred to keep silent. Thus, he kept quiet out of a sense of "reverence," opting for a "distanced" exposure. Thomas's behavior toward Chrysostom is even better known, as well as reserved. When Chrysostom states that the "Blessed Virgin Mary was not preserved from all sin," Thomas's judgment becomes more and more severe in the course of his different writings, ending, finally, by bursting out: "Chrysostom has gone too far." Harsh words, indeed, for such an author, but he shows that the authority of the Fathers is not unconditional.

We cannot mention every instance in which we see Thomas criticizing his sources. But it should be noted that the three rules discussed above guide Thomas's general attitude with respect to them. We find the same thing not only with respect to the Fathers, but also with ancient philosophers and other sources, Arab or Jewish, and even with medieval theologians. We cannot stress enough how important they are, since he applies them to dozens of authors. Again, we must recall two complementary things. On the one hand, Thomas's sources do not come only from famous personages; we also have to mention all of the more or less known authors that he gathered together in the *Catena aurea* ("Golden chain"). On the other hand, we should stress Thomas's remarkable familiarity with the history of the councils. This is important because, with the councils, the authority is no longer that of such and such a Father but of the Church, and is thus endowed with a greater authority. Here again, Thomas proceeds with a certain hierarchy: if he mentions twenty-seven different councils in 241 passages, 184 passages concern the first great ecumenical councils. It is interesting to note that "Thomas seems to have been the only great theologian of the thirteenth century to have used, as such and with a certain insistence, the dogmatic conclusions and the patristic records of the first five ecumenical councils (M. Morard).

After the Fathers and councils, one must quickly point out a last type of source, that of the medieval theologians. Rarely named, often referred to by a simple *quidam* (certain), these authors clearly do not have the same weight as the earlier authors; they are his teaching confreres, who sometimes belong to the same generation as Thomas. It is enough to recall the quarrels that his teaching caused in order to be edified. Here there is a new common convention that dictates Thomas's judgments: the teachings of theologians are not "authentic," they are not real authorities, they are simply "lecture" notes that have no more weight than the master who formulated them. Thomas is not embarrassed at pointing this out: "This gloss is simply from a lecture; it has little authority." These judgments are sometimes written in more detail, but apply to all. Even Peter Lombard himself, the master of the *Sentences*, does not escape. Thomas discusses at length Lombard's thesis on the uncreated nature of charity and establishes the contrary in an indisputable way. He also knows how to remain just and appreciates the weight of an argument. In speaking about Hugh of St. Victor, he can thus say: "Even though his *dicta* be only those of a master and therefore do not have the force of an authority, we can still use them profitably...."

These several examples will suffice to prove our point: they show clearly that Thomas respects his sources while maintaining a certain freedom. Everything that does not directly touch on revealed sources is not subjected to any other judgment than that of the truth. We will find at one and the same time a similar attitude of respectful welcome with a critical vigilance regarding philosophers, even if the Christian faith sometimes demands that we keep our distance from them.

Philosophical Sources

We said it from the first lines of this chapter: for Thomas, it is legitimate to make use of the "authorities," for example, philosophers in theology, as "foreign arguments that have only relative value." This warning does not stop him from approaching these eminent witnesses of natural reason with an obvious methodological sympathy.

We will begin with a fact that is too often overlooked but which, however, is clear: Thomas's interest in the thinking of philosophers is particularly seen in the small dossiers that precede the examination of larger problems with which he dealt. Thus, with respect to the eternity of the world, he takes care first of all to recall the opinions of the ancient philosophers on this question. He begins with the poet-theologians, Orpheus and Hesiode, continues with Plato, Democritus, and Socrates, then with Empedocles and Heraclitus, returns to Aristotle and Plato, continues with Simplicius, the Neoplatonist, and Alexander of Aphrodisias, the Aristotelian. Aristotle himself had started this inventory. Thomas was not afraid of pursuing it beyond what the earlier thinkers had done.

All of the major questions—philosophical or theological—touched on by Thomas in his writings are thus clarified by recalling different positions. The best example of a discussion informed by what he learned from history on a specific subject is found in *Separate Substances*, in which Thomas's enquiry goes on for seventeen chapters (thirty pages in the Leonine edition). Etienne Gilson considers this book as "one of the most typical Thomistic writings: attentive to everything that the philosophical tradition can offer him," remarkable especially by the "information that he takes advantage of" and that reveals "a "fully mature researcher . . . , in full possession of his method."

Thomas's interest was not limited to Greek and Latin authors; he also availed himself of Arabic-speaking philosophers. We have counted 405 explicit references to Avicenna (980–1037), a Muslim-Persian philosopher and doctor who wrote in Arabic), 503 references to Averroës (already mentioned in our discussion of the unity of the intellect), and 205 Arab or Jewish authors other than Avicenna and Averroës. Thomas is familiar with Maïmonides (who also wrote in Arabic) for his reflection on providence and prophecy. This is all the more remarkable, given that certain Latin translations had been quite recent.

As for the way Thomas reads these authors, we can use the example of how he understands the ultimate end of humans. If he spoke about this often, he was never more explicit than in the *Sentences*, written while he was a young man. Philosophers and theologians diverge on this issue, he notes: philosophers place happiness in the vision of separate substances, while theologians place it within the vision of God Himself. However, we can make use of solutions that the philosophers reached to arrive at discerning the truth. Thomas reviews the positions of several authors, of whom some were eminent, before proposing his own solution. The issue in this discussion is of major significance; notwithstanding, Thomas's method in this case is more important. Thomas knows how to question those authors who precede him. He does not retain all of them but rather uses some of them for his own conclusions with a clear conscience regarding the progressive character of philosophical reflection: "The ancient philosophers entered little by little and step by step in their search for knowledge of the truth."

Thomas, driven by his presumption of good will with respect to philosophers, borrows from them everything that is not incompatible with the Catholic faith, even going so far, according to several scholars, as to borrow from Aristotle a theory of divine providence. The case of Aristotle is indeed emblematic. The time has passed when Thomas could be considered a faithful interpreter of the thought of the Greek master. Philosophers have become more and more critical; they certainly recognize that his commentaries are not without value, but this does not mean that he changed Aristotle's doctrine on certain decisive points. As with his *Commentary on the Nicomachean Ethics,* guided by the Christian concept of beatitude, originating from a vision of one God, or from his *Commentary on the Metaphysics* "steeped in a sense of the *metaphysic of being* which was completely foreign to Aristotle" (J. Owens). His creationism and monotheism are no less strange to Aristotle. We have known for a long time, "Thomas baptized Aristotle" (R.-A. Gauthier). According to other authors, his idea of political science would be "a complete repudiation of Aristotelianism" (R. Bodéüs). Even those who today wish to defend a substantial faithfulness must admit that it came about by deepening and going beyond Aristotle's text.

Beyond these generalities, which would tend to diminish Aristotle in the eyes his Thomistic readers, still we have to recognize the importance of Aristotle even in Thomas's most resolutely theological treatises. Aristotle was clearly not a source for the treatise on the Trinity, but one can still show that he is omnipresent in his method, his metaphysics of being and act, his natural philosophy, his reflections on science, and his logic, which contributed greatly to the originality of Thomas's Trinitarian theology. Others have reached the same conclusion, that the major contribution to Thomas and medieval authors stems from the fact that his philosophy is, so to speak, a "koine," as biblical authors say, that is, a language and a setting of common reference. We find numerous examples that show that his philosophy considerably helped Thomas to lay bare and to safeguard the integrality of the human nature of Christ, in conformity with the dogma of Chalcedon (451), which had rightly insisted on the fact that Christ had not only a divine nature, but also and just as fully an integral human nature, ours.

It would be too long to review all of the points where Thomas distances himself from Aristotle while still using him as he saw fit, and we can notice that, contrary to the Fathers of the Church, he avoids contradicting him too openly. But Thomas will sometimes dismiss Aristotle rather brutally. For example, he refuses to follow Aristotle's psychological theory, according to which two extreme passions cannot exist at the same time in the same subject. If we were to recall this to Thomas, who maintains that the limitless joy of the beatific vision and the depth of dereliction could exist in Christ at the time of the Passion, he would drily respond that this theory does not apply in Christ's case. In his case, the submission of the reality of the faith outweighs Aristotle's authority.

This freedom that goes just as well with what Thomas borrows as with that which he rejects or modifies when the matter
is necessary, we can easily find in the case of other philosophers, as we have already seen with respect to the Fathers of the
Church. Thomas takes what is useful wherever he finds it. He
dialogues with his counterparts, and he excels at taking advantage of their disagreements before proposing his own solution.
Be they dead or alive, he changes nothing in how he operates:
the steps are the same and the conclusion is similar; research
progresses. This is not about diverse borrowings that are more
or less artificially joined together, for Thomas leaves nothing
intact in what he borrows. As it has been excellently stated: "If
one concedes that a philosophy must not define itself by the elements that it borrows, but by the mind that animates it, we will
see in this teaching neither Plotinism, nor Aristotelianism, but,
above all else, Christianity" (E. Gilson). Thomas's borrowings are
not larceny. It is a question of honoring the authors that came
before him; he learned from them and retained a lot.

In this quest, Thomas is guided by a deep conviction that he
often recalls: "All that is true, said by whomsoever, comes from
the Holy Spirit." The universality of the presence and action of
the Spirit in this context corresponds exactly to the universality of the active presence of the Word, the creator of all things.
Whatever be the shadows of this world in which the Word by
his Incarnation brought light, Thomas explains elsewhere, one
cannot say that "no mind is dark to the point that it cannot
participate in anything of the divine light. In fact, every truth
known by whomsoever is due totally to this 'light that lights up
the darkness'; for 'everything that is true, whosoever it is that
speaks it, comes from the Holy Spirit.'"

In this light, we can understand the spirit that animates
Thomas's research when he has recourse to non-Christian

authors who have come before him. When he comes across a truth said by one of them, he knows from whom it comes and does not hesitate to adopt it. This attitude expresses the consciousness of belonging to a community of seekers after truth in which disinterested mutual aid is a fundamental law:

> Whoever wants to probe the truth is aided by others in two ways: directly and indirectly. We receive direct help from those who have already found the truth. If each of these earlier thinkers found a nugget of truth, these findings joined together into a whole are for the searcher who comes after them a powerful means to arrive at the most profound knowledge of the truth. We are also indirectly aided even by those who are mistaken, for they have given to those who have come after them the possibility of revealing the truth more clearly by the more rigorous discussion that they have provoked.

Thus, when Thomas rejects certain positions of his predecessors or when he modifies them and formulates his reservations, we must always situate it against a background of gratitude with respect to them. Aristotle had already paved the way, but Thomas borrows from him without hesitation and he extends his praise of his master in philosophy.

> It is only just to thank those who have assisted us in the search of this great good which is the knowledge of the truth.... Not only those whom we judge to have discovered the truth and that we follow in our turn in communicating it to others, but we also thank those who stopped short of reaching the end of their search and whose opinions we cannot follow. Nonetheless, even those bring us something by giving us the chance to apply ourselves in this investigation. We have received from certain of our predecessors some general propositions regarding truth; we accepted some of

them, we rejected others. Even those we received also had predecessors from whom they had received and who had been the source of their knowledge. One has to love equally one and the other: those whose advice we follow and those whose position we reject. Both one and the other equally strove to search for truth, and it is in this that they aid us. Still, we have to allow ourselves to be convinced by what is the most certain and follow the position of those who arrived at truth with the most certainty.

This praise of the philosophical tradition can serve as a conclusion to this study on Thomas's attitude regarding his sources. He translates the clear conscience of the searcher's engagement in a long temporal chain without which he could not have enjoyed the intellectual capital that he receives as an inheritance. The care of establishing his arguments on the authorities of the past do not express a safe approach, nor even an intemperate use of documentation. Rather, it expresses a profound conviction rooted in and reasoned from the historicity of human thought. Thomas's relationship to his sources is an aspect of his personality that has been for too long misunderstood. The extraordinary vitality of current-day research shows the fruitfulness of this approach. Thomas is rightly celebrated for his great philosophical choices and his speculative genius. The way in which he inserted this in history is no less remarkable.

BENESCRIPSISTI THOMA

GOD WHO LOVES
THE WORLD

As we near the end of this book, it is time to offer to the reader several general glimpses of Saint Thomas's thought. Theoretically, we have the choice between two options. The first would be to begin this task from a philosophical perspective. This would consist of uncovering the great philosophical principles underlying Thomas's various writings and, from this, to reconstruct his "vision of the world," if we can thus express ourselves. Great notions, such as matter and form, act and power, the realism of knowledge, the theory of causality, and others, are not always obvious at first reading, even though they are everywhere present and their influence is quite real. Thomas did not think it necessary to highlight this, even though it is possible to do so and there are some great successes in this area (e.g., T.-D. Humbrecht). But our pursuing this course is out of the question for several reasons. First, accomplishing this difficult task successfully would require a much longer book than this one—certainly more than a few pages in one or two chapters. Then, the necessarily more abstract character of this type of approach would go directly against the simplicity that I desire for this book. More importantly, the inductive approach of such a work, which proposes to leave our created world in the hope of being with God the Creator, can succeed only, even in the best of cases, in leading to a First Principle far inferior to the God of the Christian faith, unless philosophy reintroduces a secret faith into its reasoning.

We will thus follow a second option, resolutely theological, which will justly have as its point of departure the very place at which the philosophical enterprise is obliged to stop; thus, we will follow the narrative and more concrete mode that we have been using up to the present. Even here, though, we are constrained to limit our ambitions. We do not have the pretense of presenting all of theology in a few pages. To take into account these constraints while staying on the path that we have followed until now, we will stick to the two major topics highlighted in our reading of the *Summa contra Gentiles* and found in the *Summa theologiae*: God and the world, God and man, the Alpha and Omega. We have already learned a lot about the circular movement that generally governs Thomas's thought, about the humility of his approach when he talks about the mystery of God, and about his conception of man as a free and autonomous partner of God. We can, perhaps, complete this first approach to some extent: Who is this God from Whom we come and to Whom we go, and who is this man that God desired to be his partner? And, by extension, how do we imagine their relationship?

"God Loves All That He Has Made"

Thomas justifies this affirmation for a very simple reason: if the world exists, it is because it had been loved and willed by God even before it existed. While we can love only those things that already exist, it is God's love that calls persons and things into existence. It is here that we find the point of departure for the circular schema already familiar to us. Before everything else, it must be known that, for Thomas, the first beginning of this movement, the creation, the first gift that God made us in calling us to into being, is not found simply in the First Principle postulated by the philosophers, nor even in God, without further qualification, but clearly in the Trinitarian God of the Christian faith:

> Creation belongs to God by virtue of His being, and His being is identical to His essence, which, in its turn, is common to the three Persons. Creation is therefore proper not to one of the Persons; rather, it is common to the entire Trinity.

Each Person has a particular role to play in this shared task. To explain this, Thomas appeals to a suggestive comparison with an artist in the act of creating:

> In fact ... God is the cause of things, by his intelligence and by his will, as the artisan of the products of his art. Now, the artisan works according to the idea that he has of his work in his intelligence and by the love that his will carries in advance. Thus, God the Father makes the creature by His Word, which is the Son, and by His Love, which is the Holy Spirit.

It is not only in the *production* of creatures that the three Persons of the Trinity are acting; their action continues in the movement of the return of creatures toward God. This movement comes about under the movement of the Son and the Holy Spirit:

> Indeed, just as we have been created by the Son and by the Holy Spirit, so too we are united to our final end by them. This had already been Augustine's thought when he evoked the Principle by which we return, the Father, the model Whom we follow, the Son, and the Grace that reconciles us, the Holy Spirit.

The significance of these few words defies understanding. Stressing that God made all things by His Word, Thomas makes clear the fact that God called the world into existence by a willed and considered act. Creation is not a necessary outpouring of the divine Substance, as other believers in the "exit-return" schema imagined it to be. By equally highlighting the role of the Holy Spirit, Thomas underscores again that if God created the world, it was not because He would have had needed to, nor for any other reason than Himself, but clearly in a disinterested way. Only God can act like this. While all of our human acts are motivated by a variety of reasons that are outside of us, God has no other motive than that of the diffusion of His own goodness, His own perfection. Moreover, evoking the grace of the Holy Spirit, Thomas underscores that His role does not stop at creation; rather, it also accompanies us until the end willed by God. What this comes down to is that in the immediate extension of the creating Trinity, Thomas also speaks about the divinizing Trinity. This is the first sketch of what Thomas will develop later, in keeping with the rest of Christian tradition, when he discusses the reasons for the Incarnation: God became man so that man could become God.

The comparison to the artist in the work of creating suggests another important teaching: basing himself on the general principle according to which the effect resembles the cause, Thomas affirms without hesitation that God Himself leaves His mark on His work. This leads to an extraordinary consequence. In contrast to the earthly artist, who copies, even if that reproduction is far from the original or voluntarily distorted, a model that is exterior to him, God has no other model but Himself. If, therefore, the whole of the Trinity participates in the creative act, it must be concluded that we necessarily find a trace of the Trinity in all creatures and not only in humans. Thomas calls this trace a "vestige," according to how remote it is within the diversity of creatures; in the human person, this trace is truly an "image," an image of God. There is no need to recall that this is already in the Bible. This helps us to understand a little better why we can say with Thomas that the "entire world is nothing other than a vast representation of the divine wisdom conceived in the thought of the Father," and that the "creatures are like words that express the unique divine Word."

In order to justify the title of this section, we need to recall once again that the love of God that presides over creation is an omnipresent reality at each instant. One cannot reason as if God, having long ago created the world, would become disinterested in it later. When Thomas encounters the "impossible supposition" that we find frequently in the mystics, "If God removed for an instant His power over created realities, they would instantly cease to exist," Thomas is far from contradicting it, but he does modify it:

> Creatures' being depends on God to such an extent that they could not subsist one single instant and would be reduced to nothingness if, by an operation of the divine power, they had not been preserved in being.

It is clear that this directly points to the work of the divine Word: the Father never ceases to beget His creating Word, the source of created being. The same thing holds for the Holy Spirit, who is always springing forth from the heart of the Trinity, and who is always at work in our world. This is why Thomas can testify with the same firmness that not only is the Trinity the absolute origin and the constant sustainer of creation, but He also loves this creation with the love with which He loves Himself:

> It is not only His Son whom the Father loves through the Holy Spirit, He also loves Himself and us.... Just as the Father reveals Himself and all creatures by means of the Word whom He begets, since the Word begotten of Himself suffices to represent the Father and all creatures, so too does the Father love Himself and all creatures through the Holy Spirit, for the Holy Spirit "proceeds" as the love of this first goodness by reason of which the Father loves Himself and all creatures.... The divine truth and goodness are the principle of the knowledge and love that God has for creatures.

Far from being absent, and still less a stranger to His creation, Thomas's God is personally present to each being in a more intimate way than that being is present to itself. More than once Thomas reminds us of Saint Augustine, to whom he owes so much: "But you, you were nearer to me than I was to myself, and higher to me than my highest reach." Thomas certainly does not have Augustine's literary genius. Still, he does not say something different than Augustine does, and the way in which he speaks of God's active presence in His creation is stated well enough to rouse an amazed adoration that comes from the experience of feeling this presence.

THE WAY, THE TRUTH, AND THE LIFE

Following the logic of our circular schema, we are now invited to embark on the road that returns us to God. The Trinity does not cease accompanying us, but while the starting point highlighted the Person of the Father, it is the Person of the Son who is brought to the fore, no longer simply (if one can say this) as the Word, the permanent cause of our being, but in the form by which we know Him in the Gospels, the Word Incarnate, Jesus Christ. Now, from his first word at the beginning of the *Summa*, Thomas presents Christ as the way to follow to return to God: "In his humanity, *Christ is for us the way that leads to God.*" This affirmation is repeated with the same force at the beginning of the *Third Part*, when we arrive at the moment of speaking more explicitly of Christ: "The Lord Jesus showed us in his person the way of truth by which we can attain to—in rising from the dead—the happiness of immortal life."

Why did the second Person of the Holy Trinity choose to make himself known to us in this form? Thomas knows and recalls the numerous reasons of fittingness set forth by the Fathers of the Church to justify the mad plan that led God the Word to become one of us. There is one that is particularly expressive: it was fitting that God became man in order to give us the possibility of seeing God:

> In the highest degree, the Incarnation brings to us, who are on the way to happiness, an effective aid. Indeed, man's perfect happiness consists in the immediate vision of God. [Because of the immense distance of natures, this thing could seem impossible, but] the fact that God desired to join Himself to human nature in Christ demonstrates clearly to humans that it is possible to be immediately united to God by the intellect, in seeing Him without an intermediary. Thus, it was fitting to

the highest degree that God assume human nature in order to rekindle our hope for happiness.

Of course, Thomas does not ignore the major argument of the Fathers of the Church according to which "God became man so that man could become God." He also stresses the fact that the Incarnation is, so to speak, God taking us by the hand (a *manducatio*, he writes) to lead us on the path to God. This is the "new and living way," of which the Letter to the Hebrews speaks (10:20):

> [Saint Paul] shows how we have the confidence to come near, for Christ by his blood inaugurated, began for us a new way. It is the way that leads to heaven. It is new, because before Christ, no one would have found it: "No one goes to heaven except the one who descended from heaven" (John 3:13).... The way is living, it always lasts, because of the fact that it is seen in the fruitfulness of the divinity who lives always. What is this way? The Apostle is more specific when he continues: "beyond the veil, his flesh." Just as the high priest of the old covenant entered into the Holy of Holies through the veil, so too if we want to enter the sanctuary of glory, we must pass by means of the flesh of Christ, which was the veil of his divinity. "You are truly a hidden God" (Isaiah 45:15). It is not enough to believe in God if one does not believe in the incarnation."

This desire for happiness, the explicit theme of the "way," runs through Thomas's work. Better still, we will again find in this context that circular movement, the fruit of which we will discover more fully. Thomas's repetitiveness should cause us no fear, since it stresses the central character of his intuition:

> From the moment when God became man in assuming his nature, it is no longer inconceivable that the created intellect

can be united to God by contemplating His essence. It is thus that the entire work of God is when man, created last, returns to his starting-point by a kind of circle, being united to the very principle of everything by means of the Incarnation.

In discussions that once took place concerning the schema of the *Summa*, Thomas was reproached for giving God [the Father] an excessive role, to the detriment of Christ. This is completely unjustified. Thomas does not throw Christ to the side. He places him exactly where He must be: at the heart of our history, at the junction between God and man. Not as a static middle, but as the way that leads to the heavenly country, as "the author and perfecter of our faith" (Hebrews 12:2), who draws us after Him to the Father with the irresistible force that animates His own humanity. In one of those summaries for which he has a talent, Thomas connects this new role assumed by Christ in His eternal role as the Word in the Trinity:

> The first principle of all things is the Son of God: "All was created through Him" (John 1:3). *This is why He is also the original Model whom all creatures imitate, as the true and perfect Image of the Father,* from which the expression in the Letter to the Colossians (1:15): "He is the Image of the invisible God, the First-born of all creation, for in Him all things were created." In a special way He is also the exemplary model and fulfillment of all spiritual graces with which spiritual creatures shine, according to what is said to the Son in the Psalm (109/110:3): "from the womb before the dawn I have begotten you in the splendor of the holy ones." Since He had been begotten before all creatures by a resplendent grace, He has in Himself in an exemplary fashion the splendors of all the holy ones. *Still, this divine model was far from us.... This is why He wanted to become man in order to offer to man a human model.*

If Thomas sees in Christ the exemplary realization of all of the virtues, it is because He is the incarnate Word, who, in His eternity, already reigns over the creation of all things. This last sentence again opens a double way for our reflection. We could insist on the work of God operative in us: from baptism and by means of the other sacraments, we are interiorly modeled, formed again in the image of the well-beloved Son by the grace that He mediates. It would take us too far afield to follow this path, but we cannot forget that it is only on this basis, and with the certainty that we have become new creatures, that it is now possible for us to imitate Christ and to follow Him. This consists, first of all, in listening to Him in order to receive His message and to contemplate all that He has done to draw from His message the best spiritual part: "By His manner of life, the Lord gave everyone an example of perfection in everything that belongs to salvation." In a previous chapter, we have already discussed all of the virtues that Jesus taught by his example in everything that He did. We also did not forget that this example culminates in His passion and death on the cross. There is no reason to go back over this. Here, it would benefit us to read another passage in which Thomas describes another facet of the infinite richness of the example that Christ offers us:

> Christ had already taught his disciples many things regarding the Father and the Son, but they still did not understand that it is to the Father that Christ was going and that the Son was the way by which they would go. Indeed, it was difficult for them to go the Father. It is not surprising that they did not understand! For if Christ in His humanity was well known, they understood His divinity very imperfectly....
>
> I am Way, the Truth, and the Life, answers Jesus. At one and the same time, He reveals the route and the end of the route.... The route, as we have seen, is Christ. This is

understandable, for it is by Him that we have access to the Father (Ephesians 2:18).... The way is not far from the end, it touches it; this is why Christ adds: the Truth and the Life; He is at one and the same time both: the route according to His humanity; the end according to His divinity....

The end of this route is the fulfillment of all human desire. Humans desire two things above all else: one that is proper to them, namely, the truth; the other that they share with everything else that exists: to remain in being. Now, Christ is the way by which we arrive at truth since He is the Truth ...; He is also the way by which we have life, since He himself is Life.... Thus Christ called Himself the way and the end; He is the end, for all the objects of our desires come through Him: the Truth and the Life.

If, therefore, you seek the way, go through Christ: He is the Way. Isaiah (30:21) prophesized: "This is the way, follow it." As Saint Augustine says: "Pass through the man to arrive at God," "It is better that you limp along the road than to stray purposefully to the side." Even if progress is slow, those who limp on the good road draw nearer to the goal; those who walk outside the route distance themselves even further the more they run faster.

If you are seeking where to go, bind yourself to Christ: He is the Truth that all of us desire to reach.... If you are looking where to rest, bind yourself to Christ, for He is Life.... Bind yourself to Christ, therefore, if you desire to be safe; you cannot stray, for He is the way. Those who bind themselves to Him do not walk in the desert, but on a well-laid-out road.... Likewise, you cannot be deceived, because He is the truth and teaches all truth ... no more can you be shaken, for He is Life and gives life.... As Saint Augustine repeats, when the Lord says: I am the Way, the Truth, and the Life, it is as if he were saying: Where do you want to go? I am the Way. Where do you want to go? I am the Truth. Where do you want to dwell? I am the Life.

LOVED WITH THE LOVE
BY WHICH GOD LOVES HIMSELF

On the road where we go forward in Christ's wake, we are, like Him, accompanied by the Holy Spirit, the third Person of the Trinity. For Christ, that is obvious, but it is also true for us. Even if the Spirit comes in the third place, this Person of the Holy Trinity is not of less importance than the first two. First of all, it goes without saying that the Spirit is always at work in cooperation with the two other Persons of the Trinity. The Spirit is present at the creation of the world as in its continuity, just as the Spirit is equally present in the work of divine governance. If the Spirit is already there for purely natural things, the Spirit is equally and with more reason present when it comes to the work of grace. According to an expression much loved by Thomas (he uses it one hundred fifty times in all of his work), "the grace of the Holy Spirit" is at the heart of the new Law brought to us by Christ:

> The most important thing in the new Law, that in which is found all of its strength, is the grace of the Holy Spirit given by faith in Christ. The new Law is principally made up of the very grace of the Holy Spirit given to Christ's faithful.

Even if He is not mentioned, the Spirit is structurally present always and everywhere each time that there is a question of one or the other divine Person:

> United to the Holy Spirit, we have access to the Father by means of Christ since Christ works through the Holy Spirit.

And this is why everything that is accomplished by the Holy Spirit is also accomplished by Christ.

It is not enough to say that Christ and the Spirit cooperate closely in the work of the Father; rather, it is the three Persons acting together; thus, for example, if our filial adoption is the communal work of the Trinity, each Person brings its own proper touch, as in the creation:

> Even though adoption is common to the entire Trinity, it is nonetheless appropriate to the Father as its author, to the Son as its model, to the Holy Spirit as the One who stamps in us the resemblance to the model.

Thomas is inexhaustible when it comes to the Holy Spirit. Since we cannot say everything about the Holy Spirit, we will retain two of the roles attributed to Him in the Gospel; the first is that He is the Spirit of truth. When Thomas wishes to shed further light on the role of the Spirit with respect to us, he establishes a parallel with that of Christ and specifies first the complementarity of Their missions. He applies this in particular when writing about gospel teaching. Not only does the Spirit complete and recall Jesus' message, He provides us with its meaning. Without the Spirit, this teaching would be impenetrable—absolutely incomprehensible and, therefore, useless:

> Just as the sending of the Son had as an effect to lead us to the Father, so the mission of the Holy Spirit is to lead believers to the Son.... The Son, being the Word, brings us His teaching; the Holy Spirit enables us to receive it. Thus, when Jesus says: "He will teach you all things," it is therefore this: Even though a person learns from outside, if the Holy Spirit, from the inside, does not give him an understanding of it, it's a waste of time: "If the Holy Spirit does not live inside the heart of the listener, then the doctor's discourse is in vain."

This even means that the Son, speaking with the organ of His humanity, is powerless if He does not operate from the interior by the Holy Spirit.

The one who is not taught by the Spirit learns nothing; which is to say: the one who receives the Holy Spirit from the Father and the Son, that one knows the Father and the Son and goes to them. The Spirit makes us know all things, inspiring us and leading us interiorly, and raises us to spiritual things.

We can see the immediate consequence flowing from this necessity of the presence of the Spirit of truth. It is not only the little circle of apostles who find themselves implicated in these words, it is also all of those who, after them, desire to follow Christ in order to understand, with different meanings of the word, and to make the Word of God heard. To highlight this, Thomas appeals to an intimate experience led by the Holy Spirit and compares the revelation that God makes of Himself to the confidence that one makes to one's friend:

Here is why the Lord could say to his disciples (John 15:15): "I no longer call you servants but my friends, for I have said to you everything that I have heard from my Father." Since it is the Holy Spirit who makes us friends of God, it is therefore to Him that we must attribute the revelation of the divine mysteries to us. "What eye has not seen, what the ear has not heard, what has not been imagined by the human heart, what God has prepared for those who love Him, God has revealed to us by the Holy Spirit" (I Corinthians 2:9–10). And since it is from what we know that we are able to speak, it is thus necessary to attribute to the Holy Spirit [the fact that] we can speak of the divine mysteries. . . . As we say in the Credo with respect to the Holy Spirit: "He spoke through the prophets."

In laying out little by little all of the properties of God's friendship, which He maintains with us through the Holy Spirit,

Thomas moves us from the revelation of divine intimacy to its complete unfolding. Every authentic proclamation of the Word of God comes not only from the inspiration of the prophets—which is true differently and in various degrees—but also from the public proclamation of the Church down to a friendly conversation between friends. Without this prior contact in the faith of the Spirit of truth, which is its source, what we present as the Word of God would simply be nothing but words.

The second role that we must highlight when it comes to the Holy Spirit is that He is the Spirit of love. These things are tightly connected, and it is difficult to speak of one without the other. All of the gifts of God are given to us by the Holy Spirit, Thomas underscores, since the Spirit is Himself the Gift of God. This means that the Spirit gives Himself when we speak about Him as the Spirit of love. Faithful to his way of explaining the most profound things by the simplest comparisons, Thomas appeals to our own experience of gift:

> The first gift that we give to the person we love is love itself, which makes us wish for the other's good. *In this way, love constitutes the first gift by virtue of which are given all of the other gifts that we offer him.* Consequently, the Holy Spirit comes from God as Love, He comes in His capacity as the first Gift.

These few lines, which disclose to those who wish to welcome them the depth of one of our most familiar gestures, reveals the role of the Holy Spirit at the heart of the Trinitarian intimacy and what results from it for us. It is not we who have loved God, but God who loved us first. Since nothing from the outside can move God either to create the world or to be interested in it, it must be that this movement is found within God Himself. Only that love by which the Father loves the Son and by which the Son loves the Father, and which is the Person of the Holy Spirit, can explain this "exit" of God outside of Himself. Thomas is explicit: "the Holy Spirit, which is the Love by which the Father loves the Son, is also the Love by which He loves the creature and shares His perfection with him." We are loved with the Love by which God loves Himself."

We could go on and on with this truly dizzying conclusion. But at least we should give it its true dimensions. Certainly, we are personally concerned, but the Love of God is too vast to limit itself to our own little persons. The Holy Spirit is also given to all who believe in Jesus. How does this happen? Here, Thomas compares the Holy Spirit to the "heart," which waters the entire body, or to the "soul," which joins all of the members in unity. Through charity, the love of which the Holy Spirit is the source and which He gives to each personally and to the entire body, accomplishes in their midst the same work of love that He exercises in the heart of the Trinity from all eternity. The ecclesial community is an image in progress of the communion within the Trinity.

This pale reflection, full of promise, we call the "communion of saints." When commenting on this phrase of the Creed, Thomas explains: "The one who lives in charity participates in all of the good that is done in the entire world." This phrase, which Thomas uses again and again, sometimes appears in a more developed form:

> [The efficacy of prayer supposes, of course, that we desire to pray for others, which is still primary,] it is unity of charity given that all those who live in charity and form, as it were, one body. As such, the good of one redounds to all in the same way that the hand or some other member is at the service of the entire body. In this way, every good that is done by one holds true for each of those who live in charity.

In order to help us to understand the way in which charity effects this mysterious communion, which makes us interdependent beings with everyone else, Charles Journet uses a startling comparison: giving one's eyes to someone who would not have them otherwise would certainly give him a finite perfection; these precise organs of flesh would also be at the same time a spiritual introduction to the infinity of the horizon. To give him the capacity to see would also be offering him the possibility of appropriating for himself, in some sense, the immensity of the exterior world, allowing him to enter into a union with it in a new way.

Charity, likewise, has two faces. As a created reality, an effect brought about in me by the Holy Spirit, charity perfects my spiritual being, and it is necessarily limited to my person. In this sense, charity cannot explain the mutual communion for which we seek to account. If we consider that this finite charity allows me to communicate with the infinite charity, which is the Holy Spirit and which lives in me (since the Holy Spirit gives Himself at the same time as the gift), then everything changes. Since Charity at its heart thus puts me in communication with the world of all other persons in whom it is present, since it is nothing other than uncreated Love, both unique and identical, which fills the whole Church and makes of it a unity. Present in the whole of the ecclesial Body and in each of its members, the Spirit achieves a reciprocal dwelling of all those who are in a state of grace. If the Spirit of love lives in me and if I live in the Spirit, by this fact alone all those in whom the Spirit lives and who live in the Spirit also live in me and I in them. It is to this extent that we must proceed to account for the mystery of the communion of the saints. My charity does not only extend to my brother; it is his, and his is also mine. Charity communicates the resources and fecundity that it has received from the Spirit in such a way that the charity of the weakest is bolstered by the charity of the strongest, and the charity of both of them is taken up in the whole-hearted charity of the entire Church, for it is the charity of uncreated, indivisible, and omnipresent Love that all possess in common.

According to a saying that goes way back to ancient Greece, "between friends, everything is in common." Euripides said this long before Plato and Aristotle, and Christians did nothing more than follow in their footsteps. In defining charity as God's friendship with us and with all those who are friends with Him, Thomas gives to this longing coming from the dawn of time its supreme fulfillment.

BENESCRIPSISTI THOMA

WHAT IS THE MOST NOBLE IN THE WORLD

I f it is permitted to take one's inspiration from Saint Thomas even to the way in which he made the transition between the *First Part* and the *Second Part* of the *Summa theologiae*, then surely there should be no hesitation in connecting this chapter with the previous one. Let us recall this text:

> Man, being made in the image of God . . . , is gifted with intelligence, free will, and the power of autonomous action. We must, after discussing the Exemplary, God [in the *First Part* of the *Summa*], addresses what concerns His image, man, in keeping with what he is himself, namely, the principle of his own actions because he possesses a free will and the mastery of his acts.

After having "stammered" (this is Thomas's expression) for several pages about the mystery of God, we must now attempt to say something about the human mystery. It is more accessible, for certain, but it would require a thick book, and we only have a few pages at our disposal. There are some aspects of this mystery that seem most important for us to highlight. First of all, what do we mean when we speak of human beings as the image of God? It is at once a gift, a grace, but also a promise, a task to undertake. It is, therefore, necessary to inquire about the real world in which human beings, becoming God's image, work to succeed at this calling. Beyond these generalities, we will try to see how this human being becomes, little by little, a Christian (which is another way of speaking about an image that grows in its resemblance to its divine model). Finally, we will speak about the way that this unique image does not become itself except in relation to a multitude of other images, also unique, for God's plan is to bring together, into a unity of His communion, His children, whom sin has scattered far from Him.

THE IMAGE OF THE IMAGE

Here, as elsewhere, Thomas places Holy Scripture at the top of the sources for the theologian. Now, he reads, from the beginning of the Bible, God's declaration: "Let us make man in our image and likeness" (Genesis 1:26). We have to keep carefully in mind the prescriptive force of this teaching. It is not simply a way of speaking. To say that the human being has been created in the image of God is to state the reason, the final cause as philosophers would say, of the creation of man. God made humans *for* this, *so that* man would be in His image. Thomas sees simultaneously the work and the action of God and His objective: God in the act of creating man is moved with the intention of communicating His likeness to him.

Thomas is as much at ease in conforming himself to this biblical teaching as he is when it comes to his own reflection, which already leads him in this direction. When he speaks of God's creation of the world by comparing it to the creation of a human artist at work, Thomas makes this major distinction: while the artist can only reproduce created models, even simply imagined ones, God has no other model but Himself. What He created bears His mark, a divine mark, and is therefore like Him in a certain sense. Even if it is only a trace of the divine action, of which no creature is deprived, Thomas simply talks about a "vestige"; when Thomas refers to human beings, he explicitly speaks about an "image" of God. What does he understand by this expression? A first response is found in the passage that appeared at the beginning of this chapter. If the essential is indeed found there, Thomas intends to go further in his work of understanding the faith. When asked why he speaks of the image of God when referring to humans while in reality talking about the prerogative of the Son, the second person of the Trinity, Thomas answers with the following distinction:

> The image of someone can be found in one of two ways: either in a being of the same nature, as the image of the king is found in his son; or in a being of a different nature, as the image of the king is found on a coin. Now, it is in the first way that the Son is the Image of the Father; and in the second only that humans are in the image of God. Thus, in order to indicate this imperfection of the image, in the case of humans, we do not say without some nuance that they are the image of God, but are "in the image," and by this we mean the effort of a tendency toward perfection. Of the Son

of God, on the other hand, we cannot say that he is "in the image": He is the perfect image of the Father.

This nuance is particularly enlightening. The idea of a reality that is given not in a finished state, but that is called to progress, corresponds to Thomas's conception of nature, which certainly has the property of a stable base, but with the rich potential of a fulfillment to come. Humans are not fully themselves except in their finished state; just as the image of God within them will not fully be itself except at the stage of the perfection of its spiritual nature. It is not sufficient to claim that humans do not resemble God in their corporeal condition (this would lead to a really insufficient idea of God); we have to add that it is not about a static reality either, but rather a dynamic reality that is found at the superior level of the activities of knowledge and love, which characterize the human being. If humans are, properly speaking, an image of the Trinity, this means that they are endowed with intellect and will and, therefore, one can discover in them as in God the equivalent of a thought object (Thomas uses a "verb") conceived by reason and a love that is directed to the loved object and that grows in nobility according to the quality of the thought and loved object. In order to suggest this evolving character of image, Thomas applies a gradation of ascending conformity that opens the way to an infinite growth:

> The image of God in man can thus be verified according to three degrees. First, in that man has a natural aptitude to know and to love God, an aptitude that is found in the very nature of the spiritual soul, and that is common to all human beings. Second, in that man knows and loves God in fact even if imperfectly; this means image through conformity by grace. Third, in that man knows and loves God in fact and perfectly; this means image according to the resemblance of glory (in the beatitude). Thus, in margin of Psalm

4:7: "The light of your face shines on us, O Lord," the gloss distinguishes three kinds of images: that of creation, that of the new creation, and that of resemblance. The first of these images is found in all human beings, the second in the just alone, and the third in the blessed alone.

It is clear that "these three aspects of image are intimately connected to each other as three moments of the same spiritual itinerary" (A. Solignac). Thomas constantly proposed degrees as a way of understanding the image: one presupposing the other and brought to completion in the next. This clearly indicates that this dynamism of image is one of his major interests for theological consideration: "There are two ways of being conformed to the image of Christ: one in the life of grace and the other in the life of glory, the first being a path to the second, for, without grace, one cannot reach the life of glory."

We can still say a lot more regarding man as the image of God; in order to be completely faithful to Thomas's central intuition, we must add at least this. If the doctrine of image has such an importance to us, it is because it allows us to understand how the formulation of the "exit" and "return" of Thomas's circular schema is achieved in the creature, and his schema serves as a common thread for us. If the first [degree], the image of creation, is at one and the same time the term of the "exit" from God and the point of departure of the movement, the second, the image of our re-creation according to grace, is that by which the "return" to God begins, starting the movement that will end in the heavenly city with the third, the image of glory, finally a perfect true likeness. It is only thus that one gives the internal momentum of the image all of its force by resituating it within the infinite and much larger circular dynamism that brings back all of creation to God.

The whole of creation—and specifically human persons who enter consciously into this process—finds itself thus taken and led into the movement of the Trinitarian relations. We can confirm this in the icon of Trinity by André Rublev (in the form of a rectangle at the bottom of the altar, which symbolizes the created universe): creation is not outside but is, rather, at the heart of the Trinitarian communion. The genius of the painter connects with the intuition of the theologian without knowing it and makes visible something of this "movement" (this *circulatio*, says Thomas) that leaves the Father through the Son and returns to Him by and in the Spirit, leading the universe in His love.

GRACE DOES NOT DESTROY NATURE

The journey of the image of God ends in eternity. On this side of death, this image is in the process of becoming. Thomas does not forget this and suggests a more complete vision of the situation of human beings in this world. It is rightly one of his main contributions to Christian thought: that he taught theologians to distinguish between that which belongs to the structural order of the nature of things and that which belongs to the utter freedom of the divine gift. Before anything can be said regarding the supernatural plan, there are basic natural givens that one should not forget. They condition the way that the gift of grace itself is received and lived. According to an old Scholastic adage, the repetition of which, in more or less appropriate situations, has not succeeded in trivializing it: "Grace does not destroy nature, but leads it to its perfection." This is really a fundamental choice. Nowhere does Thomas conceive of man or the world in an idealistic way, as if man had only a life of the spirit, and as if the world were simply matter without any relationship with him. He always sees them as mutually linked together such as God has made them, with a nature that sin has not destroyed and that grace can take up without destroying it.

Contrary to an outrageously pessimistic spiritualizing vision that sees in humans and the world only the ravages of sin, Thomas professes a deep optimism and resolutely affirms:

> As bad as human beings can be, they are never totally deprived of God's gifts, and it is not God's gifts that one has to reprove in them, but that which comes from their malice.

We will never read in Thomas that earthly things are evil in themselves; rather, he affirms the contrary:

> Of themselves, creatures do not turn away from God; they turn to Him. . . . If they turn away from God, it is the fault of those who use the gifts in a foolish way. Whence the words from the Book of Wisdom (14:11): "Creatures have become a snare for the feet of humans without wisdom." Moreover, the very fact that they can distance themselves from God proves that they are from God, for they cannot thus attract humans except by virtue of the good to be found in them and that they have received from God.

Thomas knows well that there are persons who can "renounce the world" because of a personal vocation; but he refrains from making this kind of renunciation a norm applicable to everyone and tries to better clarify the matter:

> Humans find themselves between the realities of this world, where their lives unfold, and spiritual goods, where there is eternal happiness, in such a way that the more they lean in one direction, the more they distance themselves from the other, and vice versa. *To embed themselves completely in earthly realities to the point of making these the goal of*

their existence, their reason, and their moral choices, is to turn away completely from spiritual goods. God's commandments forbid such a disorder. Still, it is not necessary to renounce the world completely in order to achieve this end, *for one can attain eternal happiness all the while using the goods of this world as long as one does not make them the goal of one's existence.* Whoever entirely renounces the goods of this world will reach happiness more easily. It is in light of this that the evangelical counsels are given.

We can consider this text as a charter that is applicable to the situation of the image of God journeying towards happiness. Human beings owe it to themselves to act in such a way that they never cease moving toward this final end, even while giving themselves to the numerous tasks that they face in this in-between situation. The background of this situation is Thomas's conception of creation. This notion is at one and the same time that of a believing theologian and that of a believing philosopher, which leads Thomas to assert the autonomy and value of created reality. This created reality, truly willed by God in order to show forth and communicate His goodness, is also for Himself such that creation has its own stability and laws. The created world is not a theater where Christians would be merely passing figures; rather, it is the place where God's saving will sets right and leads to its end His creative will, with the real cooperation of humans in a unique history of salvation, the saving character of which does not do away with profane reality.

What emerges from this intrinsic value of the created universe is that human action can give itself precise objectives that, without being the final end, are still intermediate ends that are worth being pursued for themselves. To enumerate one or the other according to the important natural inclinations that are found in every human person, here is a list: to establish a family, to raise children, to search for truth, to pass on knowledge through teaching, to expand it by means of research, to struggle for a better distribution of the goods of the earth, to serve one's country by political engagement or humanity by maintaining peace at the level of interpersonal relationships, and so on. All of these objectives represent so many true goods that deserve to be explored and served. Far from leading us away from the final end, they orient us to it and allow us to serve it better.

The Christian who is involved in similar tasks pursues the mission of the humanization of the earth confided to us by our creator, according to what we find in the *Book of Wisdom* (9:2-3): "By your word you made the universe, by your Wisdom you formed us to have dominion over the creatures that you have made, to rule the world in holiness and justice and to exercise judgment in rightness of heart." Christians, therefore, have no reason to evade these tasks or to perform them halfheartedly or reluctantly. If it is about the private life of each one, they are impelled, certainly, by the necessities of life and, moreover, they have the assurance of thus working for the realization of their own proper Christian being. If it is about a public task, the fact of giving oneself for the purpose of a better society confers on this work a quality that only a believer can give it: the imitation of the divine liberality, which gives in a way that is far more effective insofar as it is completely disinterested.

The Joy of Good Works

In this world where our spiritual destiny unfolds, the human being represents a singular case; he is not simply a spirit, an intelligence. He is also an animal. He lives this spiritual destiny in a human body. Even if the image of God is found in his soul, the human person "is neither his body nor his soul"; he is a composite that results from the union of body and soul. The soul is, undoubtedly, the noblest part by virtue of its spiritual nature created by God. But it is not a complete substance existing for itself. Thomas states this with the greatest clarity: "Neither the definition nor the name of person is fitting for him." Elsewhere, Thomas uses this striking formula: "*my soul is not me.*" Man is the human person, and, here, Thomas does not hide his admiration: "The person signifies that which is the most perfect in all of nature . . .". In fact, revelation confirms this dignity, since one of the reasons for the incarnation of the Word was precisely to reveal to us its grandeur: "If God became man, it was to teach us about the dignity of human nature."

We understand this option without difficulty. In the face of any "spiritualizing" notion of human beings that runs the risk of despising the human body, Thomas's solid realism leads him to affirm, with ease of mind, that humans are corporal beings and that, without the body, there is no longer a man. But from this results a formidable difficulty. Man, being who he is, his animal nature, with all of its weakness and passions, is always far from representing a harmonious aide in becoming a Christian. Each one of us experiences this every day: the body and its desires lead us on the path of ease rather than down a road that would be better. This is why certain philosophers, who saw these disordered tendencies, spoke about the passions as "a sickness of soul." Thomas refuses to enter into such a discussion; he provides another definition of the passions and proposes at the same time a solution that is more in keeping with the idea of a human being:

> If we call passions simply movements of the sensitive powers
> of the soul and nothing more, then the perfection of the
> human being implies that even the passions are governed
> by reason.

For Thomas, it is unquestionably a question of reason enlightened by the Word of God, informed by the divine Law, strengthened by grace, and deploying all of the virtuous resources at his disposal. Understood in this way, reason is the connection of the divine plan to humans. The obedience of the sensitive powers to the rule of reason is thus something other than the submission to the narrow ideal of an exact mediocrity and the narrow-mindedness of the human soul left to itself. In fact, [reason] is the opening of the man-image to the resemblance that his divine Model presupposes. We can, therefore, better understand Thomas's conviction that the "perfection of the human good" is brought about, not by the elimination of or despising of the passions, but by their rectification and their integration at the level of the life of the spirit: "Since the senses can obey reason, it belongs to the perfection of the moral or human good that the passions of the soul themselves are ruled by reason."

What is at stake is the complete recognition of the fact that the human being is not simply the soul, he is also the body and thus equally the senses. By virtue of the unity of the substantial form of the human composition (we have already spoken of this; it means that the soul is at the same time sensate and intelligent), the movement of the senses cannot be strangers to the life—properly speaking—of the subject. These movements can become good or bad according to whether they will be subject or not to the superior faculties, namely, intelligence and the will. They are not a negligible quantity; it is with everything he is that man goes to God. A creature of God, man must be shaped by gospel values even in this part of himself in order to be able one day to arrive at the divine resemblance to which he is called.

It is here that we encounter one of the most original parts of Thomas's theology: his teaching on the virtues. This must be clearly understood. Virtue is not a shackle imposed on nature in order to discipline it, in spite of itself, under orders and precepts to which it can only resist; rather, it is a supplementary perfection that moves in the direction of its true end, since, by reason of its creation by God, nature is fundamentally oriented to the good. In applying himself to the ordering of his actions, and notably in the instinctive domain of the passions, whose divergent impulses risk destroying him, man takes upon himself the work of God to achieve the completion in the most perfect way possible of the humanization of his being by means of his freedom. Human nature is not fully itself except by cultivating the virtues.

Virtue is a way of acting for the purpose of achieving the good and performing good actions in a habitual way, such that the person who does such actions not only does the good but betters himself and is made good as a result. While most of the time our acts are aimed at "doing" (making) something, virtue consists in "acting" in a good way (living). This distinction between doing good and acting in a good way is capital if we are to distinguish between knowing how to do something and virtue. This adds the idea of moral perfection. We could say that virtue is necessary for human beings not simply in order to become good, but to continue to live well. It is not enough to know the good by means of reason, one also has to do it: virtue proceeds from the will. It is here that we return to the passions, for insofar as the senses can obey or not, they are susceptible to becoming the subject of the virtues. Temperance, for example, has the task of disciplining our basic tendency toward that which attracts us by teaching us how to resist everything that distances us from the good by training against easy pleasure. Fortitude, moreover, has the task of strengthening our courage to confront obstacles in the face of all that could turn us away from the good either by fear or laziness. In both cases, virtue strengthens the person in his attachment to the good, while the fact of succumbing to natural downward movement of his passions could lead him to disintegration.

We begin to see how virtue renders good those who exercise it. To contribute to preventing the ruination of the moral being and unifying deeply even his sense powers already represents a gain. We should also mention an additional benefit often left unnoticed. While a contrary act provokes sadness, since it is the result of an exterior violence that is often imposed, the virtuous act is, on the contrary, a source of joy. This is the direct consequence of the ease with which we utilize virtue; far from diminishing the value of the act, the pleasure with which we accomplish it grants us, on the contrary, both ease and merit:

> The more the subject operates with joy, which is a sign of the virtue, the more his acts will be lovable and meritorious.

Thomas says this again elsewhere:

> Actions virtuously accomplished are naturally loveable. The joy that we take in them belongs necessarily to the virtue and is a part of its definition. *We are neither good nor virtuous if we do not find joy in acting well.*

Clearly, we are at some distance from the pious slogan that was so widely used in the past: that which costs us is the most meritorious. We cannot necessarily conclude that we should not act out of duty but only for pleasure, but it is certain that if we were to act with at least a little love, we will find in it our joy.

Here, we can add—and this is far from an aside—that there is an "intelligent" use of virtue that excludes all narrowness. It is not only sadness that virtue eliminates, but also cowardice. Among the qualities of the virtue of courage, there is also what

we call magnanimity, the greatness of the soul. The consciousness of one's littleness before God does not eliminate one's consciousness of greatness. Is there any need to underscore this?
This harmonious exercise of virtue is not acquired except by a
lengthy apprenticeship. From the carnal roots of our beginnings
to the moment at which the image that is in us will become similar to its divine Model, the road passes through a long conquest,
that of the spontaneity of our virtuous attitudes.

To stay in the line of the valorization of the attitude that
God expects from man, we have purposely left aside an entire
plan of the doctrine of the virtues—those virtues that we call
theological—that God gives gratuitously by His grace, because
they have God as their object and are out of bounds for our
natural abilities: faith, hope, and charity. Far from being without
a relationship with the corporeal origin of the acquired virtues,
they crown it and bring to all of the virtues an unexpected aide
to human reason alone.

WITHOUT FRIENDS,
WHO WOULD WANT TO LIVE?

To this question, which he encounters in his reading of Aristotle, Thomas responds with the same conviction as Aristotle: in
whatever situation or at whatever age we may be, "friendship
is that which is the most necessary to live." For one as for the
other, it is a question of a fundamental option, and it encompasses chosen friendships between two persons as well as the
whole of familial, social, and political life, but, for the Christian, it encompasses also a fullness of meaning that one could
not have found in Aristotle. For Thomas Aquinas, the *philia*
of Aristotle is translated by the word *amiticia*, which we call
"friendship." If the word has for him all of the resonances that

Aristotle ascribes to it, especially the idea of communion centered on the common good, it also has other meanings that stem from the Latin tradition, and Thomas will transfigure the Latin word *amiticia* by defining charity as a friendship between God and man. The authority for this reference is no longer that of Aristotle, but St. John (15:15): "I no longer call you servants; I call you *friends*." Aristotle continues to furnish the structure of the definition, but the elements of it are radically changed, since the good around which this communion is established between God and man, and among human beings, is the divine life communicated by grace.

Here, we will leave aside interpersonal relationships, which are part and parcel of any discussion of friendship, in order to better focus our attention on the social dimension, which is essential for completing the vision of human beings according to Thomas. He never thinks of man in the individualistic terms that we have valued in our Western civilization for a long time now. Thomas always sees us as participating in the community of the "called"—whether we refer to is as Church, People of God, Community of the Faithful of Christ, Communion of Saints, or the Mystical Body of Christ—without ever abstracting it from the larger human family of which we are members by virtue of birth.

Thomas takes from Aristotle that humans are "beings destined by nature to live in community," which we often express as "a naturally politically animal." If it happens that this is not the case, such a person must enjoy a humanity superior to that of regular people, as did certain holy hermits, or depraved individuals, or less than human. For Aristotle, who is citing Homer, such a person has neither clan, nor law, nor home, and Thomas comments: he is "'asocial,' since he has no link to a friendship, 'illegal,' since he does not submit to the yoke of the law, 'scoundrel,' because devoid of reason.""

Preceded by the conjugal relationship—since the first of all communities is that of a man and a woman—and by family—since the family follows immediately after the union of the man and the woman—the political community, which represents a prior stage of human life in society, is nevertheless first by nature. It subordinates itself, therefore, to the communities prior to itself, and does not destroy them, for they give witness, even though to a lesser degree, to that which impels humans to live together, which Thomas, in the line of Aristotle, states as follows:

> In fact, we see that if certain animals have a voice or a cry (*vox*), humans alone have a language (*locutio*).... Human language serves to signify that which is useful and that which is dangerous, and therefore what is just and unjust. The word is therefore proper to humans for, by comparison to the animals, it is proper to [the former] to have the knowledge of good and evil, of the just and unjust, and other realities of this kind, which can be signified by the word. Now, it is precisely the "communication" of these values that constitute the family and the larger community; humans are therefore by nature a domestic and political being.

This "communication" belongs to the members who take part in the values and the goods that bring this community together. Thus, we move beyond a simple exchange in matters of justice or injustice and move to a convergence of all of the members of the community regarding the goods that are common to them. In these conditions, to say of humans that they are political animals, or better yet, social, does not mean the simple brute tendency of a more or less gregarious instinct; rather, it points to the capacity for virtuous development needed for life in society.

The good life in society supposes, in fact, that all of its members are ordered to the same common good. And this is why a society needs a leader, chosen by the community, and why it is governed by a common law that focuses on creating a collection of general conditions for the purpose of facilitating exchanges, communications, and finally friendship between the members in such a way that each person reaches his or her own end while respecting others and that a genuine solidarity makes it possible to pursue the common ideal. From this perspective, there is no opposition between private goods and the common good, for the "common good is the goal of each person living in community," and, therefore, "the one who seeks the common good of the many, also seeks his or her own good as a consequence."

Individualism is so rooted in us that we are not used to this language; for Thomas [this understanding of the common good] is obvious, and he explains that the reason why this is so is that the relationship between the person to society is that of a part to the whole, a member to the body:

> The part [as such] is something of the whole. Now, man is
> in society as a part is in a whole; all that he is belongs to the
> society.

Whatever it may cost our egos, the good of all is paramount, for according to Aristotle, it is "more divine than that of a single individual." This phrase, over which a lot of ink has been spilled, can be understood as long as one adheres to the natural level. When talking about the relationship of the person to God, Thomas uses other language. His intention, which is proper to a theologian, never abstracts from the ultimate end. Even those texts that are more obviously "sociological" cannot be taken in isolation. In this treatment, God appears for what He is: the true ultimate common good to which is subordinated all of the others:

> The particular good is ordered to the common good as to its end; the being of the part, in fact, is a being for all. From this comes [the idea] that "the good of the community is more divine than the good of the person." Now it is God, the sovereign good, who is the common good [of the universe], given that the goods of all depend on Him. Indeed, the good by which each being is good is [at the same time] His own particular good and that of all the others who depend on Him. All things are thus oriented as to their end, towards this only good, which is God.

It is clear that Thomas is careful to preserve the freedom of persons in a society. If the comparison of the whole and the part can cause fear that this dimension could be lost from sight, this simple recall of the evidence suffices to show that it is about nothing: a free man is not a common thing.

In the concrete situation in which we find ourselves, Christians come from two great societies: the earthly city of which they are members by virtue of their birth, and the Church to whom they belong by virtue of baptism. If the Church is nowhere discussed in a special way in the work of Thomas, it is for the reason that in reality the Church is everywhere in the movement of human being's return to God. We could say almost the same of the political community. There are certainly in Thomas elements of a political theory, but we would search in vain for a complete treatise on this subject. This is not the place for us to engage in this undertaking. The important thing is not so much to be complete as to perceive the major lines of the thought of the Master, who finds himself almost interwoven in the two communities: ecclesial and political. Without overdoing the comparison, we can certainly assume that just as the earthly city is the place where the natural qualities of the human being flourish, so the Church and her sacraments is the place where humans find themselves equipped for their supernatural life and where they flourish in their quality of children of God. Do we need to specify that, for Christians at least—to express ourselves in biblical terms—the loss of Eden and the passage of humanity through the experience at Babel have left to each generation, and to each one among us, a long road to travel in order to reach this ideal?

On the first page of this book, I invited you to travel with me to discover a St. Thomas who is a little bit more accessible than his reputation would have us believe. I am not presumptuous enough to believe that I have perfectly responded to your expectation.

Some of you perhaps thought that this "most simple" Thomas was still not enough. It is true that certain pages required more effort from you. I did my best, but this is neither Thomas's fault nor yours. As soon as we leave a familiar environment to discover an unknown terrain, we inevitably feel as though we are in a foreign country. It is the same for our mental state. One has to befriend this unknown and, in a certain sense, learn to navigate this new terrain. This is even more true when we try to understand realities that escape our senses, realities with which the greatest minds in every age have struggled and even legitimately disagreed. Certain chapters of this book are in this category, I admit. May I ask you to make a new effort? Reread these pages over which you have foundered. A second reading will already be much easier.

On the other hand, there are certain of you who perhaps found that this "most simple" Thomas is in fact "too" simple, even simplistic. It is true that I have not discussed all of Thomas's thought and that I willingly avoided subjects that are too diffi-cult. For an introductory study, this was not needed. Moreover, the brevity of this little book, for which I have been criticized, forced me to reduce complex reasoning to its most simple expression, to sacrifice many nuances, to leave out a number of examples that would have nicely illustrated our very condensed explanations. All of these choices were heart-breaking for me. I found solace in the words of our old Boileau, who strongly recommended precision: "He who cannot control himself can never write." To you also who still hunger, I have favor to ask of you, or rather a suggestion to make. When you have the desire (and the time), study the two volumes below (or, better, study both). It is these volumes that I have tried to condense into this book and from which I borrowed much:

Saint Thomas Aquinas Volume I: The Person and His Work, 3rd ed. Translated by Matthew K. Minerd and Robert Royal. Washington, DC: The Catholic University of America Press, 2023. In this volume you will find more historical details on Thomas's life, on the dates of his writings and their content, as well as a number of works that have been written about him.

Saint Thomas Aquinas, Volume 2: Spiritual Master. Trans-lated by Robert Royal. Washington, DC: The Catholic University of America Press, 2003. This volume offers a more theological approach and is vastly more complete than that which we have sketched out in the two final chapters of this book that you have just read.